A NO-HOLDS-BARRED GUIDEBOOK

aimed at white women who want to stop being nice and start dismantling white supremacy

It's no secret that American society encourages women to be nice, polite, and conflict-avoidant. These might be good rules for casual conversation, but when it comes to addressing racism, they only serve to uphold the status quo: white supremacy.

As the founders of Race2Dinner, an organization that facilitates conversations between white women about racism and white supremacy, Regina Jackson and Saira Rao have noticed white women's tendency to maintain a veneer of niceness and strive for perfection, even at the expense of antiracist work. What's the way through this? Confronting and deconstructing niceness—from tone-policing to weaponizing tears—and posing tough questions along the way. After all, has being "nice" actually helped Black, Indigenous, and other women of color to overcome the barriers of racism? Has being "nice" helped white women in their quest to end sexism, or to gain economic parity with white men?

White Women is a call to action to those of you who are looking to take the next steps in dismantling white supremacy—your white supremacy. Your capacity to handle conflict is the only thing that will bring about real equity. It may be uncomfortable, but without discomfort, we have no chance.

More Praise for

White Women

"Deconstructing white women and white supremacy has never been more necessary than it is right now, and I am always looking for ways to learn, grow, shut the F up, and listen. This book gives you the tools to do just that."
—Chelsea Handler

"I am excited for what this book means for us all. In a world where critical race theory is banned in classrooms across the USA, because the white people were not properly taught to think critically about their complicity in systemic oppression, this book is timely. We tend to tiptoe around whiteness, and this book rips the bandage off. This is the book many BIWOC have been needing to give to the white women in our lives; from our white coworkers to our white mother-in-laws, this book is no-holds-barred. This is the answer to many of our prayers."
—Prisca Dorcas Mojica Rodríguez, author of *For Brown Girls with Sharp Edges and Tender Hearts: A Love Letter to Women of Color*

"Delivering clear and deliberate messaging, *White Women* enables white women to understand how our overt civility and desire to be nice above all else directly equates to racial avoidance and upholds white supremacy. It is the invitation you didn't realize you needed: accept it!"
—Jo Lorenz, writer and cofounder of *The Progressivists* social media network

"The rawness and realness of these dinners and experiences, the wisdom, and quite frankly the courage Saira and Regina have, has the potential to be some of the most transformational work we have seen in this space in the last few years. The setting is genius, a perfect way to set the stage for the intimacy and radical honesty needed for this work. I felt every story. As a Black woman who facilitates similar conversations in my work with organizations, I know it's necessary to have these frank conversations. But the way Saira and Regina approach it, there is little room for the participants to hide from the truth. Even with all the heaviness, it's an easy and entertaining read. I believe anyone and everyone interested in this work should read this book."
—Michelle Saahene, speaker, coach, and community leader

"This book is a sharply defined lens through which white women who consider themselves allies need to see themselves, especially if they have any hope of stopping their patterns of harmful behavior toward Black and brown and Indigenous folx of color, truly divesting from whiteness, and actually taking action in the fight against racism and white supremacy. I hate how necessary and important this book is, but for the white women who are willing to read with open hearts and ears, Saira and Regina tell it exactly like it is. If and when white women are ready to commit to racial justice, they need to move quickly beyond performative wokeness and graduate from fragility, and this book is a foundational text for that master class."   —Tina Strawn, author and activist

"*White Women: Everything You Already Know About Your Own Racism and How to Do Better* is the book that will change the narrative. Regina and Saira approach the topic in a way that is not meant to placate the reader, but to challenge them to change. This is different than most who choose a warm and fluffy tone. They deconstruct the narrative that racism is normal and put accountability back in the hands of those who uphold the systems that cause harm."

—Madison Butler, founder, Blue Haired Unicorn

"Rao and Jackson use poignant and sharp observations with moments of hilarity to highlight the institutional barriers we have to overcome to become a better society as a whole."   —Abby Govindan, comedian

PENGUIN BOOKS

WHITE WOMEN

Regina Jackson was born in Chicago in 1950 and remembers an America where everything was in Black and white. Burned into her memory are the beatings and horrific treatment of civil rights workers throughout the South; the Goodman, Chaney, and Schwerner murders; the murder of Viola Liuzzo; the murder of Martin Luther King Jr.; the murder of Medgar Evers; and the murder of President John Kennedy. The violence perpetrated on innocent people going about their lives, by white people. It is these memories that drive Regina to push for real change in America. Which is why she co-founded Race2Dinner.

Saira (NOT Sara) Rao grew up in Richmond, Virginia, the daughter of Indian immigrants. For forty years, she wasted her precious time aspiring to be white and accepted by dominant white society, a futile task for anyone not born with white skin. Several years ago, Saira began the painful process of dismantling her own internalized oppression. Saira is a lawyer by training, a former congressional candidate, a published novelist, and an entrepreneur.

White Women

Everything You
Already Know About
Your Own Racism
and How to Do Better

Regina Jackson
and **Saira Rao**

PENGUIN BOOKS

PENGUIN BOOKS

An imprint of Penguin Random House LLC
penguinrandomhouse.com

LIBRARY OF CONGRESS CATALOGING-IN-PUBLICATION DATA
Names: Jackson, Regina, 1950– author. | Rao, Saira, author.
Title: White women : everything you already know about your own racism and
    how to do better / Regina Jackson and Saira Rao.
Description: [New York] : Penguin Books, [2022]
Identifiers: LCCN 2022018964 (print) | LCCN 2022018965 (ebook) |
    ISBN 9780143136439 (paperback) | ISBN 9780525507970 (ebook)
Subjects: LCSH: Anti-racism. | Women, White—Attitudes. |
    Women, White—Race identity.
Classification: LCC HT1563 .J33 2022 (print) | LCC HT1563 (ebook) |
    DDC 305.8—dc23/eng/20220503
LC record available at https://lccn.loc.gov/2022018964
LC ebook record available at https://lccn.loc.gov/2022018965

Printed in the United States of America
6th Printing

Set in Warnock Pro
Designed by Sabrina Bowers

Some names and identifying characteristics have been changed to protect the
privacy of the individuals involved.

Contents

What Is Race2Dinner?

Race2Dinner was founded in 2019 as a dinner experience with Regina Jackson, a Black woman; Saira Rao, an Asian woman; and eight-to-ten white women. There is no better place for honest conversations than at the dinner table. Breaking bread together helps to facilitate conversations around white supremacy, racism, and xenophobia.

These dinners require white women to participate in direct, difficult conversations. It is not for the faint of heart. It is not "Racism 101." It is tough, vulnerable, and full of emotion.

So, too, this book.

Welcome.

Preface

If you're reading this, you are most likely white. Most of what's here, you already know. You've known it your whole life. After all, it's you—white people—who created white supremacy, who benefit from white supremacy, who uphold white supremacy.

A critical component of upholding white supremacy is employing a feigned ignorance that brings you here, to these pages, asking a Black woman and a brown woman to explain to you the nuances of this script; a script you wrote, directed, and produced, and from which you've amassed dizzying wealth and power. A critical component of *our* work is radical honesty. On our part, sure, but—more crucially—on yours.

Why do we bother? After all, this country was founded on the genocide of Indigenous people, the enslavement and genocide of African people. Since the beginning, it has been racism, xenophobia, violence, rinse, repeat. The Chinese Exclusion Act. Japanese internment. Operation Wetback. Jim Crow. Police brutality. ICE concentration camps. Muslim bans. The disastrous impacts of COVID-19.

All orchestrated by white people.

You know what you're doing. But you pretend not to. You've pretended for so long—decades, centuries—that some of you have managed to convince yourselves that you're immune to white supremacy, that you've been vaccinated by goodness. You believe you're colorblind. Most of you have surrounded yourselves with other white people who share your feigned ignorance. You may have the errant person of color in your friend group. Usually that person buttresses your charade. People of color uphold white supremacy every single day.* It's called being a token. We are intimately familiar with this role.

Regina retired from the Bell System in 1998 after nearly thirty years. Her position at retirement was executive director of Large Business & Government Sales & Service, reporting directly to the general manager. How did she rise to that level and accomplish those career achievements? She knew how to code switch,† how to carry herself and how not to be a threat to white people. Regina *was* a token.

So, too, was Saira—the token brown friend to countless white women. She allowed these white women to believe that their friendships with her made it impossible for them to be racist. Saira spent four decades upholding white supremacy to her own detriment, to the detriment of her family, to the detriment of all people of color.

Besides your token friend or colleague of color, you have mostly surrounded yourself with other white people. They are

---

* Even the term "people of color" is a product of white supremacy. Consider why "white people" are not considered people of color when your skin has a color, just like ours.

† Code switching is something every Black, Indigenous, and brown person knows how to do. It means changing the way we talk, emote, and behave when we are in the company of white people. It's a survival tactic.

your spouses, your neighbors, your kids' friends, your colleagues. You are cocooned by whiteness. When everything is white, you can focus on other characteristics, the things that make you different. How much time do white women spend talking about being a blonde or a brunette or a ginger?

Us? We're just Black and Asian.

When everything is white, you enjoy the privilege of not being a monolith, of not being grouped together with other white people; because you are your own unique person.

Your individuality enables you to separate yourself from bad white people: the real racists, the ones wearing swastikas, MAGA hats, and white hoods. Yes, of course, those people are horrific, violent white supremacists. But in your mind, they are not *you*; they are not even the same species as you. You would never use the N-word or call a bearded brown man a terrorist.

You are different. You are good. You are a unique human.

But us? We are a nameless, faceless Black and brown lump, grouped together.

Black people are criminals. Latinos are lazy. Muslims are terrorists. Asians are doormats. Your stereotypes of us are (a) obviously not compliments and (b) meant to keep us down, in our segmented groups, *and* separate from each of those other segmented groups so that we aren't able to effectively organize against you.

We are left fighting one another for the scraps that you (white folks) throw to us.

We are a dark mass. We even *look* the same to you. You can't and won't bother to pronounce our names. Why bother to learn the name and face of the brown woman who serves you your favorite breakfast burrito every Tuesday? Why do Randall and Richard get so annoyed when you get them confused? They both are tall Black men with beards in IT. Anyone would confuse them.

But you? You are dirty blond, whereas Beth is strawberry blond. It's Catherine with a *C* not a *K*. Your eyes are green but turn blue when it rains.

You are unique as fuck.

And this is *precisely* how you manage to detach yourself from white supremacy, in your mind. Your individuality has enabled you to create an US (good white people) versus THEM (bad, racist white people) dichotomy that lets you off the hook.

A: Define racism in the narrowest possible way. Burning crosses and epithets.

B: White people are not a monolith.

C: Therefore, those of us white people not engaging in A are not racist.

From A, B, and C, it's a short jump to D: dismissing people of color when they call out your racism, the racism of all white people, as angry, divisive, crazy, or—our personal favorite—"racist against white people."

Your white cocoon—like a real cocoon—is seamless. You aren't even conscious of this line of logic; it just happens, like breathing.

You have created safe white spaces in every pocket of your life—your home, your neighborhood, your workplace, your kids' school, your college experience, your vacation—safe white spaces that make it nearly impossible for you to see your complicity in the system that keeps Black, Indigenous, and brown people in our places, which are beneath you.

Sure, you've made quips and jokes, done things that could be considered "microaggressions," but you're not racist. That digital Blackface GIF you send around from time to time? Ribbing your Palestinian friend about being a terrorist? These are jokes. Can't people of color lighten up (pun intended)? Or what about "finding your tribe" or referring to your "spirit animal"?

You're not racist. You're the least racist person you know, right? How could you be racist?

But you are. And your quips and ribs are every bit as dangerous as the white hoods you associate with "real racism." Jabs and jokes normalize the culture that makes the white hoods possible. Plus, there is nothing funny about racism.

Do any of these situations sound familiar?

- "I don't think they were being racist, they were probably just . . ."
- Asking an Indian person you barely know what their favorite Indian restaurant is.
- Being surprised that a Latino or Black person came from money or privilege.
- Referring to a Black, Indigenous, or brown person as "diverse."
- Referring to a book that contains Black, Indigenous, or brown characters as "diverse."
- Not learning the names of the Black contestants on *The Bachelor* or *The Bachelorette*.
- Supporting sports teams with Native American names or mascots (e.g., Atlanta Braves, Chicago Blackhawks, Kansas City Chiefs).

So yes, we'll explain to you how you're racist. Even though we're pretty sure you already know, whether you're ready to admit it or not.

We'll indulge your feigned ignorance, because our lives and our kids' lives and our grandkids' lives depend on your understanding and acknowledging the truth. Our safety, our health, and our future depend on your seeing yourselves for what you are: *upholders of white supremacy.*

Or . . . dare we say it . . . white supremacists.

Before you throw this book into the recycling bin or go on a Twitter rant (or *worse*), please take a few minutes to consider what white supremacy is. Distilled to its most basic element, white supremacy is the guiding assumption that white people are superior to those of all other races. And racism is the mechanism employed by the mission of white supremacy: keeping whites at the top, at all costs. In a white supremacist society, such as the United States, white privilege is the unearned benefit one incurs from having white skin. Therefore, if you are white, you have white privilege and, in wielding and *enjoying* that privilege, you are inherently upholding white supremacy.

If any of the above makes you feel angry or upset or guilty, you are experiencing "white fragility," a term coined by Robin DiAngelo, a white woman. A common tactic used by white folks to deflect from their own complicity in white supremacy is to become defensive and shut down the conversation altogether. The impulse to center your white feelings over the reality of living as a Black, Indigenous, or brown person in America is *peak* white fragility. Even the term "white fragility" is deeply problematic. There is nothing delicate or fragile about whiteness. The invocation of such fragility—daintiness, sensitivity, vulnerability—shows us exactly how language is used to minimize white violence. It's no surprise that this term was coined by a white woman. If you insist on derailing the conversation on racism, you are actively upholding the forces of racism.

You need to know that you are not inherently "bad" for having white privilege. If you are born with white skin into a white supremacist society, you have white privilege. You didn't have a choice in the matter. That doesn't make you bad or good. It makes you human. Similarly, if you are born male into a misogynist society, like the United States, you enjoy male privilege. It doesn't make you bad. It makes you human. Just like the asshole dudes who pretend you're nuts for talking about the patriarchy, you shift into the "bad" space if you are white and you are unwilling to acknowledge your privilege.

So: acknowledge your privilege! Your unearned white privilege. Having dealt with white people for decades, we know this may be easier said than done. After all, we might even know the ins and outs of your whiteness better than you do, having had to navigate a white supremacist society as Black and brown women.

When something you read here makes you mad, makes you defensive, or even makes you cry, please practice the following: Sit with your discomfort. Sit with your anger. Think about *why* you are feeling your feelings.

And then consider this wild idea: maybe *your* feelings, right now, don't matter.

Imagine that you are the lone woman sitting in a conference room with a handful of male colleagues. One of the men becomes upset about the topic of conversation, and voices his dissatisfaction, to which another man says, "Stop being such a girl." Everyone laughs, maybe even you (just as people of color uphold white supremacy, women uphold misogyny). Afterward, you decide to tell your colleague how hurt you were by his sexist remark. Rather than engage with your valid concern, he's wounded that you've accused him of sexism. He tells you it was just a joke, that you *know* he's not sexist. And now he's the one who is freaking out. The conversation becomes about *his* feelings, rather than his sexism. Never mind the fact that you might get penalized, boxed out, or even demoted because you did something that made waves.

You made Trevor sad. And now you're the bad guy.

You know this scenario all too well. You also know his feelings don't matter, right?

So, too, when it comes to your hurt feelings around racism.

Okay, good. One more thing before we really dig in.

White supremacy means that you—white people—are raised to see yourselves as the default. In your white cocoon, you see your *white* experience as the default lived experience. The rest of us have racial and ethnic identities: Black people, Indigenous people, Indian people, Mexican people, Chinese people. *People of color.*

But white folks? You're just people.

Ergo, the term "white people" seems to enrage so many of you. We suspect some of you have already cringed at the term in these first few pages. Not all of you. We know, we know, you're not a monolith.

But until and unless you start to see yourselves as racialized beings like everyone else, you cannot even begin the process of dismantling the white supremacy that is baked into your bones.

We've been asked what we want, what specific change we'd like to see in our lifetimes. Often we'll say this: "For white people to become comfortable with being called white." Surprise and shock will often follow that response. The bar is so low, it's practically underground. Yes, this is an exceedingly low bar but one that needs to be overcome in order to even get to the meat of the real work. As long as you see yourselves as the default and everyone else as "other," there's no next step.

The next time you refer to someone as your Asian intern or Black friend, think about how often you refer to colleagues or friends or yourself as white.

My white boss. My white neighbor.

Likely never.

Please start now.

Finally, you might be wondering why we focus our work on

white women, rather than men. As Regina says, "If white men wanted to change anything, they'd have done it by now, so why bother trying to get them to do anything."

That's one reason.

Another reason: you white women have enjoyed the benefits of whiteness every bit as much as your male counterparts, and yet it is typically white men who get pegged for being the racists. White men are at the top of the food chain, the masterminds of racial violence. But you birth these men. You raise them. Sometimes you marry them. You are a critical component of the system. And you've played your part beautifully.

White men may be on the throne.

But you white women are shining it, fluffing the cushions, catching the coins that fall from their laps.

Recall that a majority of you voted for Donald Trump the first go-round. You overwhelmingly picked him over Hillary Clinton, one of your own. Why? Because Trump openly stood for white supremacy. Never mind his concomitant open misogyny. A majority of white women chose racial solidarity over gender solidarity. You know whiteness must be superpowerful if so many of you chose it for a man who bragged about grabbing women by the pussy, a man accused of sexually assaulting more than two dozen women. And what did you do four years later, after hundreds of thousands of Americans died due to his botched COVID response? *Even more* of you voted for him! White women are every bit as racist as white men. Yet we often hold white men accountable, allowing white women to skate off quietly into the white night.

What about those of you who are reflexively saying, "Not me, not me, I voted for Hillary! I voted for Biden"? We will explore this more throughout these pages but, yes, you are every bit as indoctrinated into white supremacy as those who voted for Trump. Just as being a Democrat doesn't make a man not sexist, political ideology doesn't make you immune to white supremacy. Remember, you're human.

We can personally attest to the racism of white women Democrats. In fact, it's how we came together in the first place. It all started with Saira's run for Congress in 2018. When Regina joined the campaign, she noticed the throngs of white women who were anxious to meet Saira, with the sole objective of convincing her that they weren't racist. There was a whole lot of "not me" and "not all white women." Saira accommodated these meetings for a long time. After all, she was courting voters. Saira hoped that these invitations would dry up after she lost the race in June 2018, but after landing on the radar of the alt-right media, Saira only became more visible. The white women only became *more* interested in telling Saira how *not racist* they were, and how they, *individually*, were not like other racist white women. How they were the exception.

In December 2018, Regina called Saira about one of her white friends: "Liz says she's done with you. That you calling Beto O'Rourke a white savior* was the end. That you hate white people and she's through." Regina laughed. "But she wants to know if you'll have lunch with her."

Of course.

Saira said, "How about this: I'll get some of the other white ladies who've been asking about doing dinner, we'll add Liz to the mix, and I'll do it if you'll join me."

And we did just that.

Afterward, Liz wanted to host another dinner of her own, this time with some of her white friends. So we did that one

---

* More on white saviors in chapter 9.

too. Our company, Race2Dinner—and the idea for this book— was born.

If your reactions to the pages you've read so far mirror the work we do with white women in real life, we imagine you've likely rolled your eyes, closed and reopened the book, maybe even called your token friend of color for affirmation that you are, in fact, not racist.

The pain and hurt and discomfort are not ancillary to anti- racism work, they are the guts of it. Without them, change simply does not happen. Sitting in this discomfort, a feeling you likely have never endured before, is ultimately what will break these systems of oppression. Think about it like this. If you walk into a pond, you stir up dirt in the process and it gets cloudy. Keep mov- ing, it gets cloudier. You say, "Oh, the water is cloudy. It's scary because we don't know what lies beneath." So you run back to the shore. What if you were to walk into the water and stand there and be still? It's uncomfortable because it's cloudy at first, but the water becomes clear after a few minutes because you're still. So, too, if you are willing to just be still amid murkiness and discom- fort so profound that you feel pained, you will eventually be able to clearly see the systems that are meant to be invisible. Rigid and reinforced, but invisible. You will be able to see these systems of oppression and violence. Most important, you will be able to see how you are upholding them. You cannot change what you don't see. Seeing it is foundational.

White supremacy is a toxin that poisons everyone, including white people. Keep turning the pages; if not for us and our kids and grandkids, then for you, your kids, and your grandkids.

You may not know it yet, but your lives depend on it too.

All White Women: A Note

We have heard it all and we have seen it all when it comes to the ways of white women. We often know what you are going to say before you say it.

And you don't even have to say anything.

We know your eye rolls, side-eyes, arm folds, and lip purses.

We know you center your feelings, believing that your hurt feelings around your role in upholding white supremacy—or worse, your hurt feelings when called out for your racist acts—are more important than the violence of white supremacy and racism. Your feelings often show up as tears. We call this, simply, White Women Tears. We know you cry when you are frustrated by the conversation, or feel guilty, or feel shame; and you cry to pivot the discussion away from racism and back to your hurt feelings, which, as we just mentioned, eclipse racism in your mind.

We know you use the terms "they" and "them" rather than "us" and "we" when talking about white women. This is a tactic to distance yourself from other white women who've done something problematic. For example, any one of those women in viral "Karen" videos.

In reading the preface, a good many of you have already thought, "Not me, not all white women." This is a version of what we discussed earlier, your uniqueness, your individuality, our inability to paint you all with a broad brush.

Of course, you are unique, an individual. As are each and every one of us on this planet. But when we talk about white women, we are in fact talking about you, and you, and you—ALL OF YOU.

We are talking about WHITE WOMANHOOD.

Just as all men are individuals and unique, they still all together embody the PATRIARCHY.

So as you get started here, resist the urge to exceptionalize yourselves, to set yourselves apart from the women and scenarios and behaviors we discuss in these pages. You are them. They are you.

Yes.

You. Are.

YES. ALL. WHITE. WOMEN.

We have changed the names of all the white women in the stories we relay from our Race2Dinner work. Their names are not important, as they represent all of you. In instances where we interview women specifically for this book—Black, Indigenous, brown, and white—their names remain unchanged.

As you read the anecdotes about what you do and say—and by "you," we mean the white women we discuss within these pages, and white women everywhere else—you will feel and express shock. You may even shake your head in disgust, call or text a friend to say, "I can't believe . . ." Or you might even flat-out not believe what's written here. White people expressing shock over racism is racism. It is a version of "not me," "not all white people." It is distancing yourself from the harm you all cause. It is kicking the can down the road, avoiding accountability. It is freezing, doing nothing besides being shocked.

So as you read, when you find yourself feeling shocked, don't. Instead, think about how you have acted, or act, in similar ways to the white behavior that has shocked you. This is a practice.

Drop the shock.

White Media + Money: Another Note

The people who need to start this journey more than just about anyone else are white journalists. The media is not simply complicit in white supremacy, it *actively* upholds it. We can use mainstream media coverage of Race2Dinner as an example.

First, quantitatively. The sheer amount of press we've received for our work is telling in itself: *The Guardian*, the *Today* show, and *New York Magazine*, to name a few. Why so much intrigue around an organization that fights to call out and dismantle white supremacy? Perhaps it has to do with the fact that white supremacy thrives in silence. It survives on not being called out. And when we give shape and language to structures that you would prefer to remain invisible and implicit, it's galling to the foot soldiers of white supremacy. This gall is intriguing to the media.

Second: qualitatively. The focus of almost every piece written about us has been the price of our dinners. What does price have to do with white supremacy?

Below is a social media post we wrote in response to an article about our business:

"We made the Sunday UK Times this morning in what is decidedly a better piece than we normally see at Race2Dinner. Namely, the reporter (a white woman) does not mock or insult us and actually includes a quote from a white woman who has done a dinner with us. However, the fixation with the price continues as seen in the headline: 'Ladies, your $5000 'racism supper' is ready—don't choke on the guilt.' This fixation is white supremacy—and we are tired of it. Let's break it down: $5000 split eight ways means $625 per guest. For that, they get two full hours with us, an hour with Lisa Bond, our Resident White Woman, lots of pre-dinner conversations, an open invitation to continue the discussion with any of us plus dinner, drinks and dessert. This breaks down to less than $200 per hour/per person *excluding* food and drinks. If you count dinner, the price goes down even more. If you think less than $200 for an hour of our time is comically high or a "grift" (another favorite insult we receive with regularity), you are steeped in white supremacy culture. Is $200 too much for therapy? A concert? A dinner with friends? A purse? Shoes? Yoga class? Meditation? An uber ride? Why don't you go see how much Glennon Doyle and Robin DiAngelo charge for 45 minute talks and get back to us. The fixation is racist AF."

Back when we were charging $2,500 per dinner, half of what we charge now, we received the same heat. The reality is you don't care about the amount. It could be $0.10, $10, or $10,000. Any amount for this work is too much because you see this work as charity. You doing us a favor. From that perspective, you feel *you* should be charging *us* just because you showed up—not the other way around. White supremacy culture has you believing you are doing us a favor by even caring about racism or antiracism. This results in your incessant demands that we educate you—on *your own* racism, on a system *you* created to harm us for *your* benefit. For free.

How many times in our lives have we, as Black and brown women, provided free labor for you? How many times have we been tagged into Facebook conversations where white women are "listening and learning"? How often have we been brought into boardrooms to discuss diversity? How often have we been asked to explain why something is or is not racist? And to add insult to injury, you rarely like our answer. So we are asked to explain your violence against us to you, which is traumatizing. Then we are made to endure your inevitable lashing out when you do not like to hear the truth. All for free.

Charging for these dinners is just our saying no to the free part. We're saying that our labor, as Black and brown women, is valuable. Our time is valuable. If you pay your white yoga instructor and white therapist and white hairstylist market price, why wouldn't you pay us market price? If you have a problem with this equivalency, it is racism. Pure and simple.

We deliberately chose to establish Race2Dinner as a for-profit LLC rather than a nonprofit organization. The distinction is important. We are not a "charitable" organization.

When white people think about charity or philanthropy, you consider how you can "help" or "support" others, or "be a good person." This line of thinking presumes you have amassed your wealth through intelligence and hard work. This is what we call the myth of the meritocracy. Nobody is saying you aren't smart or hardworking, but have you ever considered why and how white people have amassed exponentially more wealth than people of color? Is it that you are smarter and more hardworking than us, across the board?

Of course not.

You've amassed wealth through a system of white supremacy. You have literally made money on the backs of BIPOC. Stolen land. Stolen labor. Stolen ideas. So the notion that you want to "give" or "help" as a way of doing something good is all part of this myth that you earned everything you have through merit.

You did not.

Here's what Lisa Bond, our Resident White Woman, has to say.

"The truth is that this is work. Personal development. Professional development. Spiritual development. It's needed and necessary and worth an investment. But—and here's the kicker—if we actually think of it as an investment, we have to accept that we don't already know it all, and that we still have work to do. And, if we think of it as an investment, we have to admit that others—namely BIPOC communities—know more about it than we do. And, if we think of it as an investment, we have to be willing to want to learn and grow, as opposed to checking a charitable box that helps us 'be a good person.' And if we actually want to grow and change, we have to be willing to pay what it is worth."

So for everyone fixating on how much we charge—and why— you can understand why and how your fixation is white supremacy considering you absolutely do not do the same when it comes to other things you consider an investment: therapy, exercise, vacations, workshops, continuing education, and actual financial investments.

Here's Lisa Bond again: "Early on, I was asked nearly every single dinner: 'What do Saira and Regina do with this money?' It shocked me the first time. That didn't last long. We white women feel like we should have control over what Black and brown women do with their money. We have to ensure that it meets our 'test of worthiness.' And we do this because even though white women are told that this is a company, we haven't internalized it. We still think we are giving to charity."

One final note. We decided to write this book after more than a dozen dinners. Different white women, different dining rooms, different neighborhoods, different cities.

SAME CONVERSATION.

You are nothing if not consistently WHITE.

There are only so many dinners we can personally attend. This book is a way to share all that we've experienced—something very few have: white women, regardless of political affiliation, being honest with themselves, with each other, and with us when it comes to how they are racist. Speaking openly—and out loud—about thoughts and behaviors that you typically refuse to acknowledge to yourselves, let alone your peers; and God forbid, to Black and brown people. You have shared with us—and your dinner companions—what you perceive as your deepest, darkest secrets. Your shame. In many cases, you have had revelations at these dinners, named things you thought you didn't know about yourself—and your internalized white supremacy.

This book enables us to share all of this knowledge by reaching so many more of you than we ever could over actual dinners.

The Rules

White women love dinner parties. You love to throw them. You love to attend them. There is wine. There is cheese. There are generous ears for stories of annoying partners and sexist bosses. There are eager cohorts with whom to plan book clubs or women's marches.

Dinner parties are a white woman's safe space, in which everyone is abiding by the same rules.

Rule number 1: be nice.

Rules 2–10: see Rule 1.

This is precisely why we use dinner parties as the backdrop for our antiracism work. It would not be nice to storm off from a dinner table. In fact, it would be downright rude. White women hate to be rude. Being rude is the antithesis of being nice.

So you sit, you stay. In spite of your anger, your sadness, your guilt.

You sit in your discomfort—often for the very first time in your lives—and you listen to how you (not Donald Trump, not the

KKK, not your fathers or the founding fathers) have inflicted harm against us, women of color.

How you are racist.

Of course, Donald Trump, the KKK, your husbands, your fathers are racist. As we noted before, white men sit on the throne, oppressing everyone.

But you hold up that throne.

Because you so greatly benefit from your whiteness, you work tirelessly to protect it. In a white supremacy culture like ours, *not* working tirelessly to dismantle it is the equivalent of working tirelessly to protect it. In other words, not acting is acting.

Pretending you are unaware of your white privilege enables you to pretend you don't know that you are upholding white supremacy, which keeps the white supremacy system humming along as intended.

See how your feigned ignorance works?

It enables you to be racist—*which you are by condition*—without accountability.

And over our dinners, we hold you accountable; but more importantly, you hold yourselves and each other accountable. But first, you need to become aware of and acknowledge how your racism shows up.

It is not easy. It is not fun. But it's the first step towards extracting the toxin of white supremacy, which courses through your veins. A toxin that poisons you, poisons us, poisons the earth.

It's dinner as revolution, as revelation, as freedom.

Thank you for coming.

It's early evening in July and, because this is Colorado, it's glorious: seventy-five degrees without a hint of humidity. We pull up in Regina's car, having spent the ride over chatting about our respective days.

Regina had for lunch the best chiles rellenos the city has to offer. Saira got the family packed for their upcoming trip to visit relatives in South Carolina.

"We gonna stir some shit up?" Regina asks, smiling as she puts the car in park.

"Always," Saira responds, checking her lipstick in the mirror. Of course, the mere existence of these dinners qualifies as *stirring shit up*.

We step onto the porch and ring the doorbell. Our host, Lynn, greets us graciously, hugging Regina first and then Saira. We make a short (none of us tops five three), smiling, Black, brown, and white triangle, and then we step inside Lynn's Victorian home.

This is the drill. We always arrive a half hour before the other guests in order to get acquainted with our hosts. There are questions to be answered, nerves to be assuaged. After all, they are about to host a dinner party unlike any they've hosted or attended before.

Lynn offers us wine (yes!), queries whether we are nervous or have any reservations (no!); we ask the same of her (yes, yes, of course she's a bit scared!). She leads us back to her kitchen, so photogenic it could have its own Instagram. The aromas of saffron and garlic swirl here, there, everywhere, above us into vaulted ceilings, around a granite island, where a butcher block sits piled high with hummus, baba ghanoush, pita, and olives.

We marvel at her antique furniture and art. So much art. Sculptures even. Lynn's husband is an artist.

Two other white women appear. Elizabeth and Lauren. This will be interesting. Normally there's one host—and her six to ten guests fall roughly into her demographic in terms of age and socioeconomic background. Elizabeth and Lynn are both in their late fifties or early sixties, whereas Lauren is midthirties. There's a story here. How did this trio come together? And who will their guests be?

Elizabeth and Lauren are every bit as effusive as Lynn, all three of them doing their best to ensure we are comfortable, peppering us with questions about our concerns, our feelings.

This is all part of the pre-dinner dance. We do these dinners often, but for them, this is all new.

They are nervous.

And our presence in the kitchen is only adding to their stress. They see us as watchdogs, investigators, detectives, waiting to catch them in a racist act.

So we do what we always do, we retreat to another room and chat until the doorbell rings.

It's 6:00 p.m. sharp.

Unlike normal dinner parties, ours start right on time: 6:00 p.m. We allot two hours, and we stick to the allotment almost to the minute.

Why?

For starters, racism is a subject that white women have likely never discussed with other white women, let alone women of color. If not kept to a strict schedule, you would find a way to procrastinate all the way through dessert. Avoiding hard conversations is a staple of white culture.

Secondly, we are setting an example that our time is valuable. Women of color are always expected to provide free or discounted labor. We are expected to do more for less. And in the case of antiracism work, we are often expected to do it for free. White folks who are doing the work often see themselves as doing us a favor by even showing up.

You pay for a two-hour dinner. You get a two-hour dinner.

By six fifteen, everyone is here. Ten white women in total—three hosts and seven guests, all but one of whom are in their sixties and seventies. Regina and Saira whisper to one another, curious how Lauren, the lone millennial, got involved with this crowd.

We should pause and explain why we know so little about the dinner party attendees.

Here's the flow: Lisa Bond, the one white woman on our team, schedules the dinners and prepares the hosts. She collects payment and walks them through what's expected, which is really only two things: set the expectation that everyone has to participate while simultaneously minimizing harm to Regina and Saira.

You might be scratching your head. Harm? What kind of harm could a pack of nice white ladies inflict at a dinner party?

Just wait.

Lisa explains that if a woman cries or gets verbally abusive, the host has to instruct her to leave the dinner table immediately. When a white woman doesn't like what she's hearing, she gets mad, she gets sad, she yells, she cries. She centers herself and her feelings and consequently derails the conversation. This is the white fragility we mentioned before.

White fragility upholds white supremacy.

Therefore, white fragility is white supremacy.

Yes, centering your feelings *is* white supremacy.

This is so obvious to Black, Indigenous, and brown people but might come as a shock to you. So we'll take a minute to spell it out, using an analogy that might hit close to home.

You and your father have a fight, and it gets heated. You raise your voice. He tells you that you're acting "all crazy" again and he doesn't deal with you "when you're like this." You have had it and tell him you're sick of him calling you crazy and that he's sexist. This stops him in his tracks. He can't believe you'd call him sexist. You *know* he's not sexist. After all, he's raised three daughters whom he loves to the moon and back. And he's been a devoted husband to your mother for fifty years. Sexist? That's so mean. And a lie. And you know it. It breaks your heart to see him so sad, and then the next thing you know you are hugging and assuring him how wonderful he is. That you love and adore him. So you make up and move on to planning the next family reunion over your famous tuna salad sandwiches. His favorite.

See what he did?

He centered his hurt feelings, prioritizing them over "accusations" of sexism, and derailed the conversation on sexism. By doing so, he upheld sexism.

You do this all the time when it comes to your role in racism.

Okay, back to the dinner.

Now that everyone is here, Lynn clinks her glass and invites her guests to gather around the kitchen island, where we'll all make introductions.

Wineglasses are filled; there's a mix of hugging and handshaking. Hummus is spooned onto small plates, olives popped into mouths.

"Thanks for coming, and welcome," Lynn announces. "Elizabeth, Lauren, and I are so happy to have you—and *so* grateful to have Regina and Saira."

We smile at her, at each other, and at our guests. The good intentions of our hosts are never questioned. It takes a certain kind of white woman to want to host this dinner, to cajole other white women into coming (and paying), to put herself out here when she doesn't have to, when she's never done anything like this before.

Lynn, Elizabeth, and Lauren are no exception.

"Thanks, Lynn, Elizabeth, and Lauren," Regina begins. "Now why don't each of you go around the room, tell us your name, a bit about yourselves and why you're here."

The Civil Rights Résumé Reading commences. If White Saviorism were a course, this reading would be essential text.

White woman after white woman recites the myriad things she has done and is doing to save Black, Indigenous, and brown people.

There's the money that goes to the ACLU, Planned Parenthood, Black Lives Matter. There are antiracism books and committees to plan marches. So. Many. Marches. More than one *really* hates Donald Trump. One tears up when describing a weekly meeting she attends with people of color at a local church to discuss racism. Her parents were active in the 1960s civil rights movement. That's how she inherited her sense of right and wrong. Another is on the front lines of the abolish ICE movement. Another supports defunding the police. Some name-drop Kamala Harris. Still others name-drop local Black, Indigenous, and brown folks in Denver. Just name them, as if knowing people of color equates absolution.

We sip our wine, nibble on the pita, and listen.

The white women talk for about a half hour. Then it's our turn.

Regina smiles warmly and begins to tell her story.

"I grew up Black, poor, and active-duty military. Even though my stepfather devoted his adult life to defending his country, we were always poor, there was never enough food, no money for any new things or even for most necessities. As a child I sometimes believed that everyone lived like us. Were all army families poor, or just Black families? A lot of families were poor, but it seemed to me as a child that the Black families were the poorest of the poor. Why was that? Had we done something wrong? Did my parents miss something? I would ponder these questions often throughout my childhood. What had we done wrong to live this way and be treated how we were?"

The white women smile—warm, empathic smiles. Regina continues.

"One significant event happened that caused me not to like my stepfather, to think that he was mean and didn't care about us. As we moved from base to base throughout the country, we would always travel in our big station wagon. The only stops he ever made were at the rest stops on the interstate highways. We weren't allowed to stop at restaurants and couldn't get out to go to the restroom at gas stations. We thought he was just being mean."

A few of the white women giggle in solidarity over mean fathers and stepfathers. After all, patriarchy oppresses all of us women.

"Only as an adult did I finally appreciate that his refusal to stop for us to go to the toilet or get something to eat was motivated by his desire to protect us from your hate, violence, and racism."

The giggles come to a halt. The warm smiles are replaced by downward glances. The women look at their shoes, their purses, their pockets. They look anywhere, everywhere, but at Regina.

At 6:48 p.m., their gender solidarity gives way to racial guilt. Whiteness forces them to avoid eye contact.

Saira's next.

"I'm the daughter of Indian immigrants. Born and raised in Richmond, Virginia, taught from birth to assimilate. In Richmond, there was only Black and white—and it was very clear to me that I was to assimilate to white—not Black—culture. And boy did I ever. I went to the University of Virginia, where I joined a nearly all-white sorority, wore Laura Ashley, pearls."

The smiles slowly return at the mention of something familiar.

"I made out with white frat guys wearing T-shirts with Confederate flags who'd whisper to me how exotic I was. We all know how exotic Laura Ashley is."

Laughter. Eye contact returns.

"All my friends were white women. They are the reason I moved my family across the country to Colorado from New York when my mother died suddenly. They were my bridesmaids—and I theirs. They are my children's godmothers."

Empathy returns. Gender solidarity returns.

"They are no longer speaking to me. Why? Because I stopped being one of them. I stopped being one of you. I stopped being their token. Nobody has broken my heart like you all have."

The smiles evaporate again. These dinners often play out like a game of smile–and–eye contact peekaboo. They come and go, come and go, come and go.

Regina breaks the silence with a tap of her wineglass. It's almost 7:00 p.m.

"Let's sit down," she says, motioning to the impeccably set table one room over.

The white women file into the adjacent dining room, silent, a morose processional having replaced the huggy, happy, high-fiving gaggle from just half an hour earlier.

Regina and Saira take opposite ends of the long, wooden, antique table. We are told the flatware is Victorian-era sterling! That the piano in the neighboring sitting room is an 1890 Steinway grand. The window treatment boasts a portion of a curtain from one of the "great European opera houses."

We marvel.

"Everything I have is inherited," explains Lynn. She doesn't know the half of it.

Lynn instructs everyone to serve themselves. She took such pains to impress us with the Iraqi and Syrian food, catered by local chefs. We fill our plates with saffron rice, chicken, and salad. The dining room buzzes with compliments to the chefs, who aren't in attendance, and compliments to Lynn for her taste.

We find our way back to our seats quickly and refill our glasses.

"This smells wonderful."

"This looks delicious."

"Raise your hand if you're racist," Saira asks before anyone's had a chance to lift their first forkful.

Blank stares. The white women look at us like we are going to eat *them* for dinner.

Several raise their eyebrows when Elizabeth raises her hand. They are openly perplexed when Saira raises hers.

"I'm anti-Black. As an Asian American, I've been trained to be this way."

More than one white woman looks at Regina and nods towards Saira with her best *oh my God, you are working with an anti-Black woman* look.

We see it every time: a white woman's tacit attempt to pit us against each other. This is one of white supremacy's greatest tools, inspiring different communities of color to be at odds rather than unified against white supremacy. Look no further than the model-minority myth, manufactured by white society to create a wedge between Asian Americans and Black Americans. In short, Asians in this country have been used to keep Black people down. The payoff to Asians? Access to opportunities that are not afforded to Black folks. Proximity to whiteness.

"We know Asians are anti-Black. We know everyone thinks they are better than us," Regina calmly says.

"I am on the receiving end of racism from you and you," Saira says, making eye contact all around, "and on the giving end of racism towards Black folks."

More nervous stares.

"So, Elizabeth and Saira are the only racist women here. Okay," Regina states. "Next question. How many of you would trade places with either me or Saira, a Black or brown woman?"

They look at each other. They look down. One or two sneak in a bite of rice. Big sips of wine are taken.

Nobody.

"Okay, gun to your head," Saira says. "You have to pick one of us. Would you trade places with me, the Indian American woman, or Regina, the Black woman?"

Guess who they unanimously choose?

Saira, the Indian woman.

"So, you're not racist," Regina says, "but you wouldn't want to be either of us."

"And if your life depended on it, you'd pick being Asian over being Black," Saira continues. "So you know the ecosystem of racism in this country. White on top. Black on the bottom. Everyone else in between."

"You know." Regina concludes, "You have always known. White people are trained to be racist from birth."

A few nod, dejected, as if they've lost their best friend. A few nod as if they're acknowledging a dirty secret. Others shake their heads angrily in disagreement.

"Not me," Karen announces.

"Me neither," Judy says. "We"—she indicates we means she and Karen—"volunteer every week for Love Colorado."*

---

* The name of this nonprofit has been changed.

We are told that Love Colorado is a local social justice non-profit.

"What does that have to do with whether or not you're racist?" Regina asks.

There are always Karens and Judys at these dinners, white women eager to showcase their exceptionalism. Karens and Judys at the table who openly brag about being white saviors.

"Well, I *know* I'm not racist," Karen huffs. "Me and my husband. We donate so much money to so many causes. This is ridiculous."

"How dare you tell us we're racist," Judy adds. "What a joke."

Trish, a retired news anchor to Saira's left, shakes her blond head and rolls her eyes so dramatically, they appear at risk of falling out of the sockets and onto her plate.

Trish and Judy make eye contact across the table.

"Did you just really do that? Right next to me?" Saira asks, incredulous.

"What on earth are you talking about?" Trish asks coyly.

"You just rolled your eyes at Saira and demonstrated your support for Judy and Karen. I just watched the entire thing. We all did, right?" Regina asks, scanning the room.

Silence. The screaming silence of white solidarity.

"And now you're gaslighting us," Saira says.

"I don't even know what you're talking about," Trish says, "this is crazy."

"And there it is. *Crazy*. We are crazy for pointing out that you just rolled your eyes at me in solidarity with Judy. That is gaslighting. Google it," Saira responds, the blood rushing to her head. Gaslighting, by the way, is a form of psychological manipulation that occurs when a person or a group of people sow doubt in a targeted individual, making them question their own memory, perception, or judgment. White America gaslights Black, Indigenous, and brown people every chance it gets, throwing our reality into question, making us question ourselves.

Regina and Saira look at each other across the table, a sea of silent white ladies separating us.

"You're so *angry*," Karen hisses.

White Woman Bingo begins at 7:22 p.m.!

Angry Black woman. Angry brown woman.

Crazy.

Not me. I'm not racist.

I donate money to the ACLU!

If we had bingo cards full of these tropes, we'd win at every single dinner.

Paging our hosts! Paging our hosts! Where on God's white earth are Lynn, Elizabeth, and Lauren? Oh yes, there they are. Sitting silently like the rest.

Lynn stands. A glimmer of hope. Will she bring order to the court? Will she make good on the most important job she has, shutting down white fragility?

Nope.

She retreats to the kitchen.

Saira gets up to follow her, while Regina turns to Elizabeth and Lauren. "Are either of you going to step in here? This is the very kind of white woman nonsense you're supposed to help get under control."

Lynn is hiding in the kitchen, arranging a cake on a platter.

"What are you doing?" Saira implores.

"Dealing with dessert."

"Why are you dealing with dessert rather than dealing with the mess out there?"

For a moment, it appears that Lynn may drop the cake.

"Oh gosh, oh gosh. I'm sorry. I'm—"

"Stop. Don't apologize. Just deal. Please. We need you."

The next fifteen minutes is a mess of red faces, furrowed brows, pointed index fingers, gaping mouths.

At Regina's behest, Lauren has kicked it into high gear, challenging Judy and Karen and Trish. She tells them that they are being textbook white women. That they are being fragile. That they are acting in service of white supremacy. She says all the things we said, but the other women don't call Lauren angry or crazy. They aren't happy, and show us as much with pursed lips, but they don't unleash on her in the same manner they did with us.

Their differing response speaks volumes, but only to those who want to hear it.

This is why we insist on having white women hosts, why we don't host these dinners ourselves. You listen to each other. You might not like what you hear, but you cannot roll out your pat, racist accusations against each other.

Lynn and Elizabeth have remained quiet, for the most part, allowing their far younger host to do the heavy lifting. It is when Lauren says, for the third time, that Karen needs to check herself and stop being so hostile that things come to a dramatic close.

"That's it. I don't need this from any of you," Karen announces, standing up, slapping both hands on the table. "Here you are telling me I'm racist, and I bet I'm the *only* person at this table who personally knows a Black man who's served time in jail."

The white women nod, suggesting acknowledgment, suggesting they agree that Karen is likely right, that she is the only person at the table who knows a Black man who's served time in prison, or at least indicating that they hear Karen, and they feel for her position. Karen is about to leave the table in triumph.

"You will recall that I'm here, a Black woman, and bear in mind, one in four Black men in America risk incarceration,"

Regina says simply. "It's foolish of you to assume that you, a white woman, are the only person here who has known a Black man who's been in jail. Saira, I think it's time to go."

It's 8:05 p.m.

It's 8:35 a.m. and Saira, having just dropped off her kids at school, calls Regina.

"What's up?" Regina asks.

"You tell me," Saira says.

So begins our typical postmortem.

"White women nonsense," Regina responds, giving her glorious laugh, one that lights up the morning, the day, the universe.

"God, I wish I had your attitude, Regina," Saira sighs. "I just couldn't believe the one at the end. Prison Patty. The gall."

"Saira, I've lived in this Black body for nearly seventy years. Nothing they do or say surprises me. White lady sitting next to me talking about how she's the only person who knows Black men in jail? Absurd, but doesn't surprise me."

"I just wonder if it's worth it. Like, what are we achieving? And to what end? Did I tell you I had high blood pressure the last time I went to the doctor?"

"That's just it, Saira, you can't let them get to you. They'll kill you if you let them get to you. And the minute this affects your health, your family, that's it. You gotta get out."

"I so appreciate you, Regina."

"I'm sitting here having coffee and am about to take Dex for a walk," Regina says, referencing her dapper dachshund.

"Gotta stop being surprised. I just have to stop. And I have to stop feeling hurt. I don't yet know how to do that," Saira says, the sadness slipping into her bloodstream, reaching the lungs, the kidneys, and the heart, which is always hit the hardest.

This conversation can be rewound and replayed the mornings after most of our dinners.

"All you can do is tell the truth. All I can do is tell the truth. The rest is up to them. You can't change what you don't acknowledge. Until and unless they want to acknowledge the truth about their racism, it's just a bunch of white lady nonsense. And we don't let nonsense fuck us up."

Regina Jackson has once again rested her airtight case.

White Women

CHAPTER ONE

Your Quest for Perfection Is Killing Us. And You.

If white womanhood is a house, your need to be perfect is the foundation.

Being perfect is the key to your happiness, to your success, to your very existence.

Perfect hair. Perfect clothes. Perfect grades. Perfect nails. Perfect weddings. Perfect bodies. Perfect adoring and supportive wife and mother. Perfect employee and colleague.

White skin.

The foundational principle of perfection in a white supremacist society like ours is rooted in whiteness. Without it, your As will never be straight enough, your MVP trophies not shiny enough, your flowery dresses a bit wilted. Of course, white skin alone doesn't render you perfect, but without it, you have no chance. White skin is a necessary but insufficient ingredient of perfection. The con, of course, is there is no actual recipe for perfection. Every ingredient is ultimately insufficient, as there is no such thing as perfection.

Your endless quest for perfection is a trap. You will never be pretty enough. You will never be thin enough. You will never be smart enough or successful enough or rich enough.

Yet white women will die trying.

Saira should know. She used to be one of you.

Saira's Story

As the daughter of Indian immigrants, I was conditioned from birth to be the white woman ideal. Sometimes the language was overt: "No, you can't go to the pool. You'll get dark." Or "Priti is pretty, so fair." But more often than not, it was coded.

"Assimilate."

"Be more American."

Of course, we knew assimilation and American meant white, not Black. Even before my parents arrived in the US, they knew the drill: white people at the top, Black people at the bottom, and they'd fall somewhere in the middle. How did they know? American television, films, and books are exported around the world. Our white supremacy is broadcast to London, Dubai, Delhi, Buenos Aires, Johannesburg, and everywhere in between. In the case of India, my parents were born into British colonialism. Even before they consumed American media, they knew firsthand that whiteness was king and queen.

Thanks to the Immigration and Nationality Act of 1965, my parents were able to leave their homeland, ravaged by the British, and seek out the "American dream." The immigration act was made possible by the Civil Rights Act of 1964, which was passed thanks to the tireless work of Black people. While they were able to come to America on the backs of Black folks, once my parents got here, they worked hard to stay as far away from those same Black folks as they possibly could. Because they *knew*.

The American dream requires assimilation.

Assimilation to whiteness.

We, of course, can never be white. But we do the next best thing: we work our butts off to be as close to white as possible. This requires us to be as close to perfect as one can get, better than those around us, even better than our white peers. Better at school. Better at work. Better at sports. Better at charm. Better at cooking, cleaning, baking, breathing.

It should be noted that our actions, as South Asian immigrants, embody anti-Black racism. Our assimilation requires us to be as anti-Black as we are pro-white. It requires not only a rejection of Black people but also a rejection of ourselves, our own brown skin, our culture. All in a desperate, impossible quest to cozy up to whiteness. This is called self-loathing, or internalized oppression. Internalized oppression is required to assimilate, to become American, to become white. The con, of course, is we are never white, no matter how hard we try, no matter how much we believe otherwise.

And boy did I try, and even believe.

It was with this deeply held belief that I wrapped myself into my prettiest Laura Ashley dress, the one with white lilies on it, and shoved pearl earrings through my earlobes, a particularly painful act of self-loathing, as I knew my ears would be infected within the hour. It was a cool Charlottesville night, second semester of my first year at the University of Virginia. My hall mates (all white) and I set out together for the most time-honored of UVA traditions: sorority rush.

Even now, decades later, I can remember praying that I'd

make it, that one of the prestige houses—Tri Delt or Theta or Kappa Kappa Gamma—would accept me, warts and all.

The proverbial warts being my brown skin.

It was with a profound sense of purpose and hope that I set out with legions of other young women down Rugby Road, the central nervous system of UVA's Greek life.

What a sight to behold. Young white woman upon young white woman, with the errant Latina, Asian, or Black woman. Every hair was in place. Every dress on point. Same with our jewelry and makeup. Perfect.

It never occurred to me to even consider rushing the Black sororities. They were so foreign, so other, so lesser, they may as well have been nonexistent. There were no Asian sororities, and even if there had been, I wouldn't have rushed those either. Being Asian was lesser than white. I was going for the gold. I was going for the white.

We arrived in groups, giggling to assuage our nerves. A few women bragged about being legacies, how their mothers, grandmothers, and aunts were Kappas or Thetas here or Pi Phis or Tri Delts there. There was no such thing in India, so I did what I always did in such situations: I smiled and nodded, happy to celebrate the advantages of my white peers. House after house after house was the same. A sea of white faces, singing, dancing, welcoming us with donuts, cookies, and hot chocolate, while whispering to a select few blondes and brunettes about joining them at fraternity parties later on for real drinks. I cracked my best jokes, laughed heartily at theirs. I hugged hard and often. I sang along loudly. It was like I was auditioning for a Broadway chorus line.

Despite my best efforts, I got cut from Kappa in the first round. I was stunned. After all, I had just graduated from a private school in Richmond, like many of the Kappas. I had been *perfect* in high school. I was captain of the field hockey, basketball, and lacrosse teams. I was student body president. I was *popular*. I had played drinking games in suburban Virginia basements and jammed out with some of these women at Dave Matthews Band concerts. Not only had we played each other in sports, it was *I* who was the star of those games. If not best friends, we were certainly friendly.

And there I was, cut from their special club. Right out of the gate. Not worthy of even a second round of consideration.

A few months later, after I'd pledged a sorority that accepted more Black and brown women than the rest (three of us my year), I ran into one of those Kappas, a brunette who was a year older than me, a former field hockey rival.

"Can you chat?" Anne asked tipsily in a dank frat house.

"Sure," I said.

We went around back, where a handful of white guys were smoking cigarettes. They paid us no attention.

"Listen, I'm sorry about Kappa," Anne said, tears already welling in her eyes.

"No problem," I responded, "I'm happy at Phi Mu. But I was confused about the first round. I thought I'd make it at least a little further."

"God, Saira," she said, the tears flowing. "We all voted you through, and then a few stood up and said, 'She's not Kappa material,' and Jenny said, 'What are you talking about. A bunch of us have known Saira for years. She's great.'"

Anne was now weeping.

"It's okay," I said, placing my hand on her back.

"But it's not," Anne said.

I knew what she was about to say. I felt sick, like I was about to vomit up crappy keg beer.

"They, they"—she trembled—"said, 'Saira is not Kappa material.'" She rubbed the skin on her forearm.

Anne said this as though I were unaware that my skin color had made me *not Kappa material* my entire life. I spent the next hour comforting Anne.

"You know I'm not racist, Saira," she said. "You know that, right?"

"Of course you're not," I assured her.

She looked up and down and lowered her voice. "It was Maggie, Ellen, and Suzanne. They were the ones."

And there it was: the white woman throwing her own kind under the bus to absolve herself.

It was them. Not me.

You always tell on each other. By design, you must. In order to maintain your perfection, others must be rendered imperfect; perfection can exist only in relief to imperfection. This system of white woman perfection creates intense competition. You're intimately familiar with this, how you stab each other in the back, rip each other apart, all in an attempt to make yourselves whole.

I didn't point out the obvious, that Anne hadn't stood up for me. Nor did she leave the room in protest. Nor did she leave the sorority altogether. Anne's silence was every bit as violent as Maggie, Ellen, and Suzanne's overt racism. But there was no time to point out these facts to Anne. I was too busy making her feel better.

I didn't realize it then, but I do now. Anne performed every act in the white woman variety show. Her friends say something racist. She remains silent. She feels guilty. She confides in a woman of color. She cries, thereby centering her feelings over the racial harm. She throws her fellow white women under the bus in order to distance herself from their violence. She now feels absolved while simultaneously remaining a part of the racist institution.

As for me, the brown woman? I play my role dutifully. I

experience the racism. The harm is exacerbated by my having to deal with the white woman's tears. It has become my job to make her feel better about her silence, her complicity in the racism.

By the time we returned to the party, Anne felt better. I felt lousy. Anne rejoined her fellow Kappas on the dance floor. I walked back to my dorm and collapsed onto my floral comforter.

Fall gave way to winter. Laura Ashley became flannel shirts, jeans, and braided belts. The seasons changed but, still, I dressed like my white peers. I listened to their music. I hung out at their bars, their frat houses. I took classes with them. They mocked me for studying all the time. I didn't have backup plans. They did.

Like a Coach saddle purse, my self-loathing was something I carried everywhere during my time at UVA. A night out in late spring of junior year was no exception. A group of us, a smattering of white ladies from different sororities, were hanging out. One was Linda, a dear and treasured friend, a woman whom I considered to be a true sister; a woman who would break my heart decades later, but looking back on it now, I realize she started to break it that night. I just chose to ignore it.

This particular evening, we were sitting at an outdoor table at the Corner, UVA's local hangout spot. The Beastie Boys' *Ill Communication* was pumping through the speakers, and strings of white lights were wrapped around the trees, supplying a hint of magic. We ordered thin-crust pizza with sun-dried tomatoes and artichoke hearts and sipped beer from cans.

I sat next to Linda and across from Kate and Amber. We chatted about summer plans. Linda and I planned to stay in Charlottesville and get jobs. Kate told us about how her mother really wanted her to spend one last summer with the family at their Martha's Vineyard home. There was a young East Asian couple seated a few tables over. Their accented English caught Kate's attention.

Kate fixed her eyes on the woman, took a swig of beer, leaned in, and giggled. "Oh my God," she said. "Amber, do you remember . . ."

Amber snorted before Kate could finish her sentence.

"Y'all," Amber whispered. "Kate and I were paired as roommates first year."

At that time, UVA randomly selected roommates for first-years. We received our assignments in the mail the summer before fall semester.

"And I about died." Amber eyed the East Asian woman. "Kate Lee. *Lee.*"

The two of them cackled.

"Yeah?" Linda asked.

"Dude," Kate said, leaning in even closer. "Amber thought I was Asian. *Lee.*"

Linda started laughing, happy to be in on the joke.

"I seriously died," Amber said. "Like, what the fuck would I do with an *Asian* roommate."

The three of them burst into laughter. I prayed for the ground to open up and swallow me whole. I hoped they would stop, move on, but they didn't. They kept looking at the East Asian couple and laughing.

"Guys." I finally managed to open my mouth. "Um. I'm Asian."

They paused and stared at me, surprised, as if I'd materialized out of nowhere.

Silence.

"Yeah, but you're not *Asian* Asian," Amber said, having scoured her mind for the right words.

But I am.

"Yeah, Saira," Kate said, "you're one of us."

But I'm clearly not.

Linda looked at me adoringly. "We love *you.*"

Love me, but what? Hate them?

The most pathetic part of this story is that their grotesque words were accepted by me as compliments. In my mind, Amber, Kate, and Linda saw me so much as one of them that they forgot about my existence during this racist, xenophobic exchange. An invisible fly on a white wall.

I was able to stay, a welcome guest at that dinner, because I internalized their words. Unlike that East Asian couple, my English is spoken with a mid-Atlantic accent. I was with a group of white sorority girls, not one half of an all-Asian couple.

What does this story have to do with perfection?

For starters, there is nothing, literally nothing, that Black, Indigenous, and brown women can do to achieve the perfection of *you*. We can be more successful at school and at work. We can have more expensive clothes, bigger houses, take fancier vacations. Yet we will always lack the foundational qualification: being white.

What do you think would have happened had I pointed out how racist Linda, Kate, and Amber were acting that night? How do you think they would have reacted? Do you think I would have remained in their friend circle? Or do you think they would have cried? Insisted that they weren't racist? That I had to know that they weren't racist! I had to know that they were only joking. If I wanted to keep my social standing, could I have been radically honest about their racism, or would I have to make them feel better? Would I have to let it go?

I would have been tossed in the trash with their worn-out Birkenstocks if I had told them the truth. In fact, a few decades later, I was summarily discarded for this very brand of honesty. But you don't just hurt us. Your need to be perfect hurts *you*. White skin is a necessary but insufficient component of your quest for perfection. Without it, you have no shot. But even with it? You still have no shot. Nobody is perfect. You know this. Yet you keep trying. And failing. You pit yourselves against each other in an unwinnable competition. This is one of many ways white men keep you on your white tippy-toes, working your butts off to outdo each other. There will always be another white woman who is prettier, funnier, richer, smarter, better in bed, better at her job, better at motherhood.

Your quest to outshine each other has created, for you, the very opposite of a community.

Back to UVA's Greek system. I want to be clear: Black, Indigenous, and brown women were erased. Just like I, as an Asian woman, didn't even consider Black sororities, these white sororities didn't really consider us. Sure, they let a few of us in, tokens who would be sure to keep quiet when their sisters mocked Asian people over dinner. And, if their Asian friend (me) didn't say anything in the face of their open racism, then they couldn't possibly be racist, right?

But it isn't as though all the white women within the Greek system were being awesome to one another. In fact, I've never in my life seen such sadistic behavior. If you enjoy sex, *slut*. If you don't hook up enough, *prude*. Or worse (in their eyes), *closeted lesbian*. You are always too fat. Or too thin. Maybe even (whisper, whisper) *an anorexic*. Your shoes are cheap, making you *trashy*. Your coat is too expensive, making you *a rich spoiled brat*. Your hair is not blond. Or it is too blond and fake looking. Or it is, God forbid, red!

Your words are a vicious sea of unkindness. Being unkind is not to be confused with "not nice." Your verbal daggers are inflicted behind the back, on the sly, so your "niceness" remains intact. It's strange that you call each other "sister" considering nothing about this scenario connotes sisterhood. This quest to be the most perfect has kept you at odds. And if you can't be in true sisterhood with each other, how on earth can you be in sisterhood with us, women of color?

So what can you do? How can you turn this ship around, the one sinking with you and us on it?

Just STOP.

Your quest for perfection is a prison—for you and for us. Walk away.

At the end of every dinner, after we have hashed out all the different ways racism shows up for the white women attendees, we ask this: Besides us Black and brown women, who do you have the most contempt for?

Confusion blankets most faces. Usually one white woman will say, "White men," before another will raise her hand excitedly, a lightbulb having gone off: "Us, us, each other!"

As soon as she says it, the rest of the table nods readily, acknowledging their shameful truth. Just like you know you are racist, so, too, do you know you are each other's worst enemies. How do you know your best friend, your "sister," has said horrible things about you? Because you've done the same to her. You've just never acknowledged this elephant in the room. The system depends on your silence, your solemn commitment to trying to outdo each other, fight each other to the death in an impossible quest for perfection.

Regina says, "You white women have to stop competing with each other."

"And you need to attempt to be in community with each other," Saira says.

"Rather than tear each other down," Regina adds.

Nearly without exception, white women accept our words on this subject without denial, without anger.

"We must," Rory, a white woman doctor in Denver, responds to our words. "We absolutely must, you guys."

"I can't remember a time when I wasn't trying to outdo my friends," Jen, a slight woman with dark curls, pipes in. "I was never good enough. I wasn't an athlete. Wasn't much of a student. My mother was blond and thin and perfect. She made me feel horrible about myself. I hated me—but mostly I hated all the girls in my class who were what Mom wished I was."

You, too, have self-loathing. This is internalized misogyny. You believe that you are inferior, as a woman. This self-loathing drives you to hate all the things about yourself that you deem to be imperfect—and to loathe other white women whom you perceive to be more perfect than you.

Start loving yourselves—and each other. And then we can talk about how you can show up for women of color. Until and unless you find your own community, you cannot learn to be in community with us.

Your need for perfection, in fact, makes it impossible to engage in antiracism work.

At every dinner, at least one white woman talks about an instance where she's been "burned" on social media for saying the "wrong thing." She's been publicly humiliated, often at the hands of a fellow white woman, who is angling to show her how much more perfect *she* is at antiracism work. Yes, you even compete in the antiracism space.

We refer to this as the White Woman Woke Wars.

This gives you the impulse to stop the work, to stop engaging. If you aren't *already perfect* at it, then you don't want to have anything to do with it. Yet if you stop the work, you can't make progress. Then there are those situations in which the critique of you is coming from a woman of color. This will hit you in a deeply uncomfortable place. After all, you are not used to having us challenge you—and on a topic we absolutely know more about: being on the receiving end of racism.

Remember our stories from above. What if we had told Anne or Kate or Linda or Amber that their words and actions were racist? Deeply, violently racist? What if we did it on Facebook for others to see? These are the scenarios we are talking about.

Us publicly calling you out on your racism.

Us publicly telling you that you are not perfect.

Antiracism work depends on your acknowledging your imperfections, namely how you have been born into and nurtured by a white supremacist society. This means acknowledging that you are not the expert on how it feels to be on the receiving end of racism, which means you do not get to decide what is and is not racist. Just like men don't get to decide what is and is not sexist. It means acknowledging that you *will* get it wrong, that you *will* feel embarrassed, and that you *will* struggle to make progress. In spite of these obstacles and this necessary discomfort, you *will* have to pick yourself up and get back into the work—work that is messy, not tidy. Work that is tables turned upside down, not neatly set.

Work that is imperfect.

You will still show up. And you'll do it because not only is it the right thing to do, but you know that your lives, and your kids' and your grandkids' lives, depend on your showing up, even when things get hard. You will show up because you understand that white supremacy hurts you too.

You are doing this not to save us, but to free yourselves.

So the next time you think any of the following:

I didn't pipe up on Facebook because I don't want to be attacked, or

I'm scared I'm going to say the wrong thing, or

The last time I called someone out at a dinner party, my husband was grumpy with me for a week,

think about this: the only wrong move is remaining silent,

sitting on the sidelines, accepting your role in white supremacy. Don't do nothing out of the fear of doing it imperfectly.

Get in there. Read. Listen. Learn. Speak up. Speak out. Show up. Roll up your sleeves.

And *when* you receive criticism, consider this: Maybe it's just that, a critique, and not an attack. Maybe this disagreement isn't a fight. Maybe you *don't know more* than the Black, Indigenous, or brown woman attempting to set you straight. And isn't freedom from white supremacy worth some level of conflict? Isn't it more important to eradicate racism than to be *liked* by everybody? You've never been liked by everybody in the first place!

Take the lead from the experts: in this case, Black, Indigenous, and brown women. Regina's advice is this: Get off social media and start having conversations with women of color in real life. You're not going to dismantle white supremacy on Facebook or Twitter, and the constant threat of humiliation online will keep you from doing the actual work off-line, in real life: engaging with real Black, Indigenous, and brown women.

The work that happens off the internet is critical. And it also involves doing something that might seem anathema to this work, which is building community with other *white* folks committed to antiracism.

"It is also one of the hardest things to put into practice," says Lisa, our Resident White Woman. "We must build a community of white people. Because most of us do not have real, meaningful relationships with Black, Indigenous, and other women of color. And how could we? Because we live in a society that is still very much segregated. Our schools and our homes, our workplaces, our places of worship are all impacted by racism and white supremacy. The thing about it, however, is before we can build a community full of BIPOC, we must build a community of white people. I'm not talking about the friends and family you already have. I'm talking about real, steady, hold-us-accountable, radically honest community. It is this community who will be there with you—not coddling and consoling, but supporting you in your antiracism journey. Your community will move you through accountability to understanding and then to reconciliation. They will hold you with care and they won't let you quit."

Beyond building a community, Lisa has a few more suggestions for divesting yourself from perfectionism.

1. Recognize reality. We all want good family photos—but does your family really need to look like it belongs in an L.L.Bean catalog?

2. Learn to appreciate what other people do, and what you are able to do. Be okay with not getting everything done. Appreciate what does get done and work on the rest later.

3. Be gentle with yourself; it will allow you to be gentle with others.

4. Have a growth mindset. How often have you told your children, "You can do hard things"? Believe that for yourself too.

5. Free yourself of judgment and allow that freedom to flow to others around you, as well.

6. Recognize that mistakes happen, and let them go. Learn from them and then move on.

7. Be yourself. You may not be everyone's cup of tea—not everyone even likes tea. But that's okay—a lot of people do.

What does this have to do with antiracism? Shouldn't we want to get it right? Of course, but perfection isn't realistic. It never has been, and regardless of what we have been taught in Whiteness 101, it never will be.

"We white women will typically have one of two responses to getting things wrong and being called out," Lisa says. "We will quit or we will self-flagellate. Now, some people think self-flagellation is 'wokeness.' You'll see and hear these comments a lot when BIPOC call out white folx; comments like 'we are so awful' and 'we're the worst' and 'we can never be trusted' and on and on. This moves into the realm of performative antiracism. Like its defeatist counterpart of 'I can't get it right so I just won't try,' self-flagellation doesn't actually *do* anything. Its primary objective is to make you *look* like the perfect white ally while not actually doing a damn thing to dismantle the systems. Both responses lead to the same result. When we are frozen by fear—of being wrong, of making a mistake—we will never be able to take the actions necessary to overthrow these systems. Whiteness is an inadequate placeholder for perfection. It always has been. Throw them both out and start over with something radical and true."

In the end, you cannot even start the process of extracting white supremacy from your being until you extract the need to be perfect.

Your need to be perfect is not just harmful to us, it's harmful to you.

Aren't you tired of never being good enough? Of cleaning your baseboards before people come over? Of spending your vacation trying to get the perfect photos for Instagram? Of crafting the most clever, grammatically correct emails? Of attempting to look younger? Eradicating your gray hair? My God, aren't you tired of trying to be thin? This particular subject matter comes up quite a bit in our work, as many of you say this is how your perfectionism has been most harmful to you, often resulting in eating disorders that you are trying your darndest not to pass along to your children.

On the subject of children, aren't you tired of making sure your kids are dressed the right way, are in the right schools, have the right piano teacher, are attending the right summer camps?

It was exhausting typing all the ways you attempt to outdo one another, and yourselves. The amount of time and energy and money you spend attempting to be perfect.

If we are tired typing it, you must be exhausted from doing it.

Your need to be perfect hurts us. And it hurts you, and your children too.

CHAPTER TWO

Your Nice Is Actually Evil.

We've established that white skin is an absolute prerequisite for white woman perfection. So what comes next?

Being nice.

"I'm a fat woman," says Lisa Bond, "so I'll never meet the thin beauty standards of a white supremacist society, but I will be the nicest person in the room. I will be so nice that I will overcompensate for what I perceive as my imperfections. You all, of course, don't have that option."

What Lisa means is that Black, Indigenous, and brown women can never fully compensate for lacking white skin. We can be nicer than Mister Rogers and Mother Teresa combined and still be seen as not quite nice enough.

And God forbid we exhibit *kindness,* which is a killer to your niceness.

Regina's Story

I was standing in the checkout line at King Soopers, and there were two cashiers, one in front of the other. Both white women. The one at the end motioned for the next customer, who happened to be a slight, older Latina woman who couldn't move forward because the white woman at the first cashier was blocking her. Let's be clear about the backdrop here. This was a time when ICE was terrorizing our Latinx communities. Just saying that. So this white woman won't move, and the Latina woman can't get past her. So I say to the white woman, "If you could move your cart back a bit, she can get by," to which she responded, "Who is going to make me? You?" Well, that was that. So I told her, "You can take your white privileged ass and go straight to hell." The overriding issue here is that it was the job of the cashiers to keep the line moving, and neither of them, both white, said one word. So I, a Black woman customer, had to ask her to have some human kindness.

Things devolved from here. She called security on me and pushed her grocery cart into me. Yes, she physically assaulted and called security on a Black woman for asking her to move out of the way for a Latina woman to pay for her groceries. My committed offense? I wasn't being nice. PLEASE. Bye, Felicia.

I sometimes tell this story at our dinners—and the white women unanimously laugh, as though the white woman villain at its center is make-believe, not one of them. But she is every white woman. I acted with kindness, in consideration of another human being. But my kindness required me to speak up and out against the white woman's behavior, which rendered me "not nice." *So* not nice, she felt the need to call security.

So you can see how "white nice" can be the polar opposite of being kind. Your definition of nice requires you to remain silent in the face of, well, just about everything. When we don't act according to your definition of being nice, namely when we speak up, immediately we are rendered not nice, or worse.

We are *mean*.

Regina and Saira recently had a call with a white woman from the New York City area who was interested in hiring us to do antiracism work within her start-up company. She spent ten minutes explaining to us that diversity and inclusion were a "priority" and that her company was "committed to creating a safe environment for *everyone*."

Her good intentions were presented. Then it was our turn. "Okay, great," Regina says, "it sounds like you've given this a lot of thought." "I have," she confirms, "yes, yes I have."

"Please know, though," Regina continues, "that diversity and inclusion isn't antiracism, and though many white people think air-dropping a few Black, Indigenous, and brown people into an organization steeped in white supremacy is a solution, it's not."

"Nor is it necessarily safe for those Black, Indigenous, and brown people," Saira adds. "Diversity and inclusion can sometimes be a lipstick-on-a-pig situation."

We hear a few deep breaths.

"Maybe if you both said things a little *nicer*, you'd get further," she blurted. "And maybe then we *white people* would be less racist."

"What?" we both say in unison.

"Your tone is just bad. It's a turnoff."

Tone. That word. We hear it *all the time*. There is a term for this: "tone policing," a way for people who are uncomfortable with the topic of discourse to silence the speaker. It focuses on the *tone*, rather than the content of our speech. By doing so, it diverts the conversation from the subject at hand. In this case, racism.

Because you cannot take umbrage with the content, because

we haven't said or done anything wrong, you take umbrage with the tone. It is a form of gaslighting.

"I think we are done here," Regina says.

"Agreed," Saira says. "When you are ready to start this work in earnest, you know where to find us."

Wouldn't you know it, a few minutes later, she emails us: "Let's agree to disagree on your methodology. I have the utmost respect for what you are doing."

A white woman entrepreneur contacts us about doing anti-racism work for her company only to tone police us. The entitlement she felt to demean and belittle us, speak down to us. And when we didn't respond the way she expected, namely we ended the communication, she insisted on making peace through more racism: agreeing to disagree.

When white people tell people of color to agree to disagree when it comes to racism, it means they are asking us to agree to their racism. What this woman essentially said is this: "I don't like what you are saying about racism, as it implicates me, so I am going to tone police/gaslight you, and when you don't bow down to me like good Black and brown women are supposed to do, then I will require you to remain silent, *make nice*, pretend like everything is fine, which also includes you not speaking ill of me to anyone ever." All of this in one pithy, poisonous statement: Let's agree to disagree.

Remarkably, in her mind, and in the minds of myriad white women she relayed this story to, *she* was the one being nice. We, on the other hand, were being mean.

Let's Agree to Disagree.

We Don't Talk Politics or Religion Here.

Watch Your Tone.

So Rude.

Honey Attracts More Flies Than Vinegar.

Do unto Others as You Want Done unto You.

Smile More.

She's Tacky.

She's Not Likable.

She's Divisive.

Is It So Hard to Be Nice?

We hear these phrases a lot. At our dinners. In our regular lives. Online. We also read them in books, watch them on TV, see them in films, listen to them on podcasts.

You hear them too. Because you say them all the time.

The enemy of this white nice? Honesty. Authenticity.

The white woman at the grocery store called security on Regina because Regina was being her authentic self, which is kind. And as we have established, being kind is often anathema to white nice. Regina's kindness showed up as asking the white woman to simply move out of the way to allow for a Latina woman to pass. That simple request instilled so much ire, the white woman barked at Regina. And then Regina did the unthinkable, she was honest, calling out the woman's white privilege. So the white woman called security. You might be shaking your head in shock and disgust at this white woman, but spare us. You do this all the time. You'll recall Amy Cooper, the white woman who called the police on Christian Cooper, a Black man, simply because he asked her to put her dog on a leash in Central Park, as required by law, and she decided she didn't like the way he made this request. You have called the police on Black people having a barbecue. You have called the police on Black children selling water. You have called the police on Black people sitting inside a Starbucks waiting for coffee. You have called the police on Black people putting groceries in their car, walking in their neighborhoods, sitting in their front yards. What King Soopers Karen did to Regina was no different.

Right now, you're likely saying, "Not me, I've never called security or the police on a Black, Indigenous, or brown person."

Yes you.

Even if you haven't called security or the police on a person of color, consider how you've treated Black, Indigenous, and brown folks who speak the truth in your presence. We would venture to bet that the white woman who contacted us about doing antiracism work at her start-up has never called security or the cops on a person of color. Is she any less racist because she has not dialed 911? You decide.

We were honest: DEI work is not antiracism work. We relayed our honesty as our authentic selves. Air-dropping Black, Indigenous, and brown folks into a white institution isn't safe. It can be a lipstick-on-a-pig situation. This woman didn't call the police on us, but she did come right out and say that if we wanted white people to be less racist, we'd have to be nicer. Which, let's face it, is what you mean when you say things like "I don't like your tone" or "if you were less angry, maybe you'd be able to get your point across."

This woman is a white liberal Democrat in the greater New York City area who called us because she is devoted to diversity, equity, and inclusion. She sits on more nonprofit, do-gooding boards than you can count, and bought every antiracism book she could find on Amazon. But the minute Black and brown women were honest with her about the problematic way in which she was envisioning DEI work, the minute Black and brown women were authentic in communicating this honesty, she became enraged.

We were not nice. We were mean. Accordingly, we deserved her racism—and all white people's racism. We see this a lot from white women. Victim blaming. We speak up and out about racism using language and a tone you don't like. We are the dictionary definition of NOT NICE.

Therefore, we deserve racism and xenophobia.

Again, you might be thinking, "Nope, not me, I'm not like that," but you are.

Below are a handful of statements we have heard over the past two years working with a large cross section of you.

"I just don't like Serena Williams, she's so rude."

"I don't hate Muslims, I just don't know why she has to make such a big deal about wearing that scarf on her head. She talks about it all the time. It's annoying."

"My God, that woman flew off the handle just because I mispronounced her name. She could've just said it more politely."

"I'm sorry, it's just not nice correcting your boss in public like that. I realize what he said was crass, but she came off even worse."

What do all of these examples have in common? They are all reactions to incidents in which your image of what "nice" looks like has been trampled.

Your dislike of Serena Williams isn't about her "lack of sportsmanship." What really gets your goat is that she speaks her mind, she doesn't smile on command, and she doesn't say please and thank you or express outward gratitude to you for her success. Why does this bother you so much? Because Serena Williams is her authentic self, which is a powerful Black woman. Her mere existence is an affront to white nice.

The Muslim woman lawyer at the firm who openly talks about how her hijab is part of her identity is "annoying." The Latina woman at the PTA meeting said, "You know, I've told you how to pronounce my name three times, maybe you could actually try to learn it," and was deemed impolite. The white man at work laughing about "cowboys and Indians" was merely "crass" and less offensive than the Indigenous woman who asked him to stop.

In every one of these cases, the offending woman of color

would have kept her nice intact had she kept her mouth shut. To be clear, no amount of silence on any of their parts could ever render them perfect. If the Muslim woman silently brought in more revenue for the law firm than any other lawyer, she would not be perfect. If the Indigenous woman silently endured her racist boss's "jokes"—or even laughed along—she would not be perfect. If the Latina woman silently smiled through your daily massacring of her name, she would not be perfect. Even Serena Williams, one of the greatest athletes of all time, could not be perfect if she smiled and bowed to her fans. Forget perfect; in each case, the honesty of these women, their authenticity, their refusal to sit quietly, has turned them into an *enemy* of white nice, an enemy of white women, who are nothing if not nice.

And when we are deemed your enemy, you will stop at nothing to destroy us.

As Black and brown women who have been called every name in the book, we can tell you this: white society does not treat loud women of color with kindness.

By that we mean slurs, insults, and threats against us, our families, and our colleagues. Violent threats against our children and grandchildren.

So the next time you decide that a woman of color at work or at the doctor's office or at the grocery store isn't being nice, rather than chastise her, slap her wrist, ghost her, talk trash about her, or get her fired, consider how your tone policing, your decision that you don't like her, your need to exact punishment upon her could result in personal, emotional, economic, and, yes, even physical harm.

Even if you would never call the cops, consider how you act like cops, policing behavior. Serena Williams doesn't genuflect at your altar with gratitude for supporting her. The white nice police—that would be you—show up to make a citizen's arrest, trashing Williams here, there, and in every mainstream media outlet in the world. The Latina woman publicly corrects your (repeated) mispronunciation of her name? The Muslim woman, God forbid, openly and proudly embraces her hijab in a culture that demonizes Islam? An Indigenous woman shuts down disgusting "jokes" about cowboys and Indians, and holy hell, she does it to your mutual boss in front of everyone? In each of these instances, you rush to the scene, a valiant first responder to police her impropriety, her rudeness, her gall.

Not calling the *actual* cops on Black, Indigenous, and brown people isn't the ceiling, it's the floor. Certainly, you can do better than that. And a great place to start is within your own alleged friendships.

Why alleged friendships?

Because we have a hard time seeing how you are truly friends. True friends are not "nice" to your face and then trash you behind your back. And this practice is a prevalent component of white women friend groups.

Not long ago, we were out to dinner and seated next to a large table filled with white women. There must have been about a dozen of you. It didn't take long to discern that this was a college friend reunion. We also couldn't help but learn that Madison and Lilian couldn't make the trip, as one had just had a baby and the other had to attend a family wedding.

Poor Madison and Lilian. The amount of shit that was spoken about each. Whew!

There were prayers that Lilian's new baby wouldn't be as ugly as her first. And wondering whether Lilian's deadbeat husband would even be able to support the family, regardless of whether the new baby was as ugly as his toddler sister. And bets placed on how drunk Madison's husband would get at the wedding, which felt hypocritical considering the white women's own wine consumption. Also, would said husband hit on Madison's sister, as he usually does?

And each time one of you would get up to go to the bathroom, the rest of you would hunch over and whisper something about the woman who'd left the table. One of you was about to get fired from work, another had gained at least five pounds. Having to pee in your friend group was dangerous!

By the time we paid our bill and left, each one of you—as well as Madison and Lilian, whose only crimes were childbirth and family obligations—had been trashed by the others.

Even the women at our dinners who have a tough time coming clean about their racism will readily acknowledge how horrible they are to each other, even to those they consider their best friends. Saira can confirm. After all, this is how she was treated by her former white friends—and how she treated them.

When you wonder how being nice hurts you, this is it. You are feverishly trying to appear to be good to each other because you know that, in reality, you are awful to one another. You don't have friendships. You don't have sisterhood. You have competition. It's like a lifelong game of *Big Brother*.

Your white nice is a cover for white rot. It cannot possibly make you feel safe and supported and loved and in community because you know what happens when you "leave the table."

Wouldn't you rather be honest with yourselves and each other? Wouldn't you rather trade in your fake white nice for authenticity and genuine kindness? Don't you want true friendships, love, and community?

And if you don't, stop penalizing Black, Indigenous, and brown women for choosing honesty, authenticity, and kindness over your toxic white nice.

CHAPTER THREE

Your White Silence Is Violence.

White woman proverb: "Talking politics at the dinner table is rude. Not in my house."

A critical component of being *nice* is being *silent* in the face of racism.

You may not be the one at your Christmas Eve dinner who refers to a Black person as "sketchy," but when you don't speak out against this language, be it from your spouse, your uncle, your aunt, your mother, your father . . . your silence is every bit as powerful as their words.

Your. Silence. Is. As. Violent. And. Racist. As. Their. Racist. And. Violent. Words.

We address this—the violence of your silence—at all of our dinners.

This particular dinner takes place in Ellen's backyard. Tables are unfolded, pushed together, and wrapped in red-and-white-checkered tablecloths. Bottles of rosé are plucked from a nearby cooler and placed on top. Strings of white lights hang from trees above. A cool September breeze inspires a few of us to pull fleeces and sweatshirts over our heads.

We choose our seats, smack in the middle, on one side. Ever since Lynn's dinner, we have committed to sitting side by side. There is safety in physical proximity, the women unable to drive a wedge between us with their whiteness.

As each of the eight white women who surround us explains why she's joined us this evening, a pattern emerges: about half have adopted Black children. These are mothers who love and adore their kids. These are mothers who know their kids inside and out, know what's best for them.

What they have not considered is that we know a side of *them* that they try not to know. How can we, strangers, know these white women better than they know themselves? you might ask. It's survival. We have to. Black, Indigenous, and brown women are experts in white women. In order to navigate and survive your everyday racism, we have had to study your every move, every pattern, every signal, every word. Just like you know men better than men know themselves, people of color know white people better than you know yourselves.

We know you'll do *that*, so we do *this*.

We may as well have PhDs in white womanhood.

You may know your kid better than we do, but we know you better than anyone and can tell you, sight unseen, that your whiteness is harming your kid. This harm is likely unconscious. That is, until it is brought to your attention, and you choose to ignore it.

Towards the end of this particular dinner, something happens that Regina cites as being the hardest moment she's ever experienced doing this work.

The two hours are coming to a close, and Janet lets out a big sigh across from us: "I've been concerned about my sister and her husband around my daughter. They've just said too many problematic things." She takes a minute, rubbing her temples in preparation for this agony: "I need to cut them off." More pausing, more rubbing of her head. "At least for a while."

"This is hard work. It means losing friends and sometimes family," Regina says. "You're doing the right thing for your daughter."

Janet nods. "Thank you. I've known this for a long time. I'm horrified it's taken this long. She's my only sibling." There is palpable anguish. "But my daughter is . . . she's my daughter. I have to."

"No you don't," a voice erupts to Regina's right. Even in the dark, we can see the blood rush to Melissa's face. Through pursed lips and carrot cake, she blurts: "You know, my parents are from a different generation and say some racist stuff around my son, but they love him, so I'm not going to alienate them. Why would I cut him off from his grandparents?"

"What happens when he gets a little older, taller, bigger, and his grandparents become suddenly scared of him, because he is a Black man?" Regina asks calmly.

Melissa rolls her eyes.

"This is real," Regina continues, her voice rising. "I can attest to this as the mother of a Black son."

Melissa folds her arms.

"Do you really sit there in silence as your parents say racist things in front of your *son*?" Saira asks.

"They love him and that's all that matters," she responds.

"You realize that your silence is unspoken approval of what your parents are saying. Your son is seeing it as approval. You get that, right?" Regina presses.

"That's ridiculous, and you both trying to convince me to end my relationship with my parents is crazy."

"What if your parents let your uncle and aunt make rape jokes to you at the age of nine? Wouldn't you be scarred for life if they didn't step in?" Saira asks. "If they were literally silent in the face of rape jokes?"

Silence.

"Okay," Regina starts. "Imagine a young girl, who is at an impressionable age . . . an age at which her ideas about gender in the world are being formed. . . . Imagine that some of her older family members make jokes around her that make light of rape, suggest date rape is not the same as 'real' rape, or diminish the importance of consent. What kind of effect could this have on her conception of rape culture? Now imagine if her parents did not intervene, or even say anything, when these comments were made."

Melissa: "That's not an apples-to-apples comparison."

Saira: "But it is."

Melissa puts down her glass.

Regina: "Please, please think about this, for your son's sake. Your silence. In your own house. In response to your own parents. His grandparents. If you are silent, you are cosigning their hateful words. You get this?"

Melissa is silent.

Saira: "Melissa, could you provide an example of something your parents have said to your son?"

Melissa shifts uncomfortably in her seat. "There is often talk about his hair. Sometimes, they'll pat his head and say things like 'can't you do anything about his hair?'"

Regina: "And you don't see how your silence here is a problem?"

Melissa is silent again. Silent about her own silence in the face of racism directed at her own child. The rest of the white women are silent too.

White silence begets white silence. We point out the layers

and layers of silence, thank Ellen for hosting us, and head home. We can speak our truth, we can point out your racism, but we can't force you into action.

We can pour a white woman a big glass of truth but cannot force her to drink.

"This breaks my heart," Regina says, pulling away from the curb. "Back when Michael was about nineteen, he would walk to work. He said to me one day, 'Mom, when people see me coming, they cross the street.' You know, it just broke my heart. He'd done nothing to these people except walk down the street as a young Black man. This woman is going to let her own parents, this young boy's grandparents, discriminate against him in his own home. Breaks my heart."

"They sincerely don't see their silence as wrong in any way," Saira adds. "It's wild. They refuse to hold themselves accountable."

"Imagine if they'd just call a thing a thing," Regina says, rolling down her window. "If they called out their openly racist fathers and mothers and sisters and bosses."

There's a saying in Germany. If there's a Nazi at the table and ten other people sitting there talking to him, you got a table with eleven Nazis.

Racism depends on your turning the other way, getting up from the dinner table to grab more rolls from the kitchen, laughing nervously, convincing yourself they didn't mean what they said, and in any event, *you* didn't say it, so you're off the hook. Racism depends on your justifying your silence: *His grandparents love him, I need this job, my husband is a good guy.*

We are at dinner in a predominantly white Denver neighborhood.

Midway through the roasted chicken and couscous, Allison

mentions a Facebook post that Saira had made a year earlier about the racism of liberal white women.

"I couldn't believe the white woman tears on that one. It was out of control," Allison says, smiling.

"I don't recall ever seeing you on my Facebook," Saira says.

"Oh, I've been a silent lurker on your page for years."

"Why don't you ever speak up?"

"It's just not . . ." Allison stops to take a sip of water. "It's just not my thing."

"Calling a thing a thing is not your thing?" Regina asks.

"All I was trying to say is that I agreed with Saira on the post. That's why I brought it up," Allison says defensively. Her attempt to identify herself as exceptional hasn't gone according to plan. She wanted to show us how she's different from the white women who'd cried foul on Facebook.

Not me. Not this white woman. Not all white women. In trying to make this case, she proves just the opposite. Allison's passivity may as well be an endorsement of the behavior on Facebook.

"You understand that silence is not support, right? That the only force that gains power from silent support is white supremacy," Saira says.

Regina shakes her head. "What on earth are you all so afraid of?"

Our host, Amanda, smiles. "You hit the nail on the head, Regina. We are scared. I'm scared."

Regina asks, "Of what?"

We look at each of them one by one.

Susan: "Of what people will think."

Saira: "What people?"

Susan: "Basically everyone."

Amanda: "We don't want to seem mean."

Nods all around the table.

Regina: "So being nice equals being quiet in the face of racism."

"Wow," Allison says. "I've honestly never thought of it that way before."

Saira: "What did you think? If not that?"

Susan: "That if I'm not saying it, then I'm not racist." She pauses. "But I think I've always known that's not true. And weirdly I feel relieved to say this out loud."

"Great, now that you have publicly stated before each other that you know your silence is racist, are you committed to speaking up?" Regina asks.

"In real life as well as online?" Saira adds.

Yes, yes, they all assure us.

This is the one dinner at which we fly past the two-hour limit. We end up staying closer to four hours, delving into all the different ways these women have been silent.

Patty's dad hates Muslims. "September eleventh did a number on him," she tries to explain. She's never confronted him.

Susan's husband uses the word "ghetto" to describe "bad neighborhoods." She's never spoken up, she says, "even though I know what he really means is Black."

Allison's boss regularly makes fun of his assistant's Mexican accent behind her back. Allison has never said a word.

There are stories of friends mocking Asian "slant eyes," brothers and sisters trashing Native Americans for wanting the R*dskins to change their name, husbands who call Colin Kaepernick a "thug."

The stories are varied.

The silence is the same.

We leave, chastising ourselves for letting the night get away from us. For overstaying.

"Well, let's see," Regina says. "Maybe the extra time to reflect on all the bullshit will make a difference."

We catch up with Amanda, our host, a few months later. She mentions that she and two of the women from the dinner have continued their antiracism work. She also talks about how she understands it is her job to engage the white women in her community.

"I realize that additional learning could and should take place through *doing*, not just listening, absorbing, and passing knowledge along. Our dinner inspired me to take on more accountability, engage and challenge the many white women I regularly interact with."

"That's the work," Regina says. "To push your friends, your family, your co-workers. Not to sit in silence thinking, but actually voicing your convictions. Out loud. In the moment."

"Yes, that dinner made me realize that I had been sitting in a place of comfort, for quite some time," Amanda responds.

White silence is comfortable for white women. White silence is harmful, and even deadly, for Black, Indigenous, and brown people.

Our Uber pulls up in front of Chloe's home a few minutes before 7:00 p.m. It's a rainy and cold Chicago evening. Chloe warmly welcomes us. She explains that her guests are all friends with one another and are evenly divided between medical and mental health professions.

Chloe turns off the oven, washes her hands, and places trays of food on a side table as everyone arrives. We do a quick round of introductions in the living room before piling salad and lasagna onto our plates and taking a seat at the dining table a few steps away.

While we are in a different city, a thousand miles from home, the scene is the same as always. Nervousness, anxiety, and excitement cling to the walls and the hardwood floors.

Tonight we go around the table and ask each woman to tell us one racist thing she has done in the past six months to a year. The nerves turn to sheer panic, and we see it in their expressions, ones we have grown accustomed to.

"Okay," Chloe says, taking a deep breath. She speaks, and then another and then another. It is the fifth woman, Nicole, who tells a story we will never forget—and that perfectly illustrates the violence of your silence.

Nicole takes a deep breath. "This was last month. I'm a nurse. I'm at work, and the head doctor of our practice gathers the nursing team to give us an end-of-year update," she starts. "He's a white man. We are nine white women. And he says, 'Our goal for next year is to hire fewer foreign doctors.'"

The rest of the dinner guests all sit up keenly, waiting to hear what happens next. "We'd hired a slew of Black and brown doctors recently, so we immediately knew what he meant."

"What did you say?" Regina asks.

Nicole takes another deep breath. "I said nothing. Not only that, I went through the whole thing in my head. Maybe I heard him wrong. But obviously I didn't. Maybe he didn't mean what he said. But obviously he did."

"Did any of your colleagues say anything? The other white women?" Saira asks.

"We said nothing. Not a single one of us. And then the meeting was over," Nicole explains.

Regina asks, "So, your silence, what did it mean?"

"My silence meant I approved of his message of racism and xenophobia," Nicole says. "The craziest part is that I knew this as it was happening, and I still said nothing."

Saira: "Why?"

Nicole: "Because I didn't want to jeopardize my job. I didn't do the right thing, and even in the moment I knew it. And this is the first time I've told anyone, and I have to say, it feels like the weight of the world is off my shoulders. I have been so ashamed."

Regina starts speaking but is interrupted by Mona, the white woman sitting next to Nicole. Mona is the mother of another attendee and is in her sixties, whereas the others are in their thirties and forties.

"Well," Mona says, "that's awful. I'd never do that."

Different city. Same white woman exceptionalism. *Not me. Not this white woman.*

"Like we said at the beginning of this dinner," Saira says, "it's all of you."

"Unless of course, Mona, you are the first white woman in the history of this country who has never been silent in the face of racism," Regina adds.

"That's true. I know I've been silent. More times than I care to count." Mona turns to Nicole. "I'm sorry."

"This is another thing. You all need to start being in sisterhood with each other. Stop stabbing each other in the back. How can you be in sisterhood with us when you are constantly throwing each other under the bus?" Saira says.

Not only is white woman exceptionalism false, but in it lies the implication that if you are the exception, other white women around you are the rule. You believe that you're better than them. How can that be healthy? How can that be sisterhood?

A lightbulb goes off, and the women collectively let out a chuckle.

"Oh my God, that's so true. We are awful to each other."

"We literally fight over men, who has lost the most weight."

"I've honestly never thought of that," Mona says. "It's been a lifetime of fighting over everything with every woman I've ever known, including my mother and sister."

"We know," Regina says. "So if you're even awful to one another, how can you even begin to be decent to us?"

We return to Nicole.

"How will your behavior change at work?" Saira asks.

"I plan to speak up. Not just at work. But also at home. In my community, which is a predominantly white one." She takes a second. "I won't be silent anymore."

"And this should be pointed out," Regina says, "Nicole's work is the perfect example of society. White male doctor at the top and a bunch of white women nurses working for him. White male boss makes racist statement. White women subordinates support him through silence. See how this works?"

There are a bunch of *oh my God*s and *wow*s.

Mona says this: "This is how it has been since I was a little girl—and nothing has changed. You both are right. We let white men say and do horribly racist things, and we put our stamp of approval on it, all while maintaining our own innocence because we, personally, aren't the perpetrators."

Bingo.

We finish dessert—chocolate cake—and call our Uber to head back to our hotel.

"Different city, same white woman silence," Regina says as we buckle up in the back seat.

"Truer words have never been spoken," Saira responds.

No matter where you go, there you are. White womanhood has no borders. Denver, Chicago, Charleston, San Francisco, New York City, Miami, Paris, London, Berlin, Toronto, Sydney, Cape Town.

And back to how your behavior, in this case your silence, hurts not only us, but also you.

You work full time, yet are still responsible for most of the housework and are the primary caregiver to your children. You are fuming at your husband, who acts like he's doing God's work by just going to the office every day. Yet you don't speak up.

You have busted your butt at work this year, have brought in a ton of new clients, yet you get a subpar performance review. You are devastated. And silent. You vow to just work harder next year.

You drive by your best friend's house on the way home from the grocery store and notice the cars of two other friends out front. You stop and peer in the window and see the three of them chatting away, wine in hand, inside. You are deeply hurt not to have been invited, but do you say as much? No way. Silent.

Your silence eats away at you. You are on and off seething at your husband, your boss, your friends, your kids' friends, their parents. All because you are not honest and authentic in the moment, choosing to be silent. On the rare occasion that you do speak up, you are called angry or crazy or divisive; this might sound familiar because it mirrors how you treat us when we speak about racism.

Your silence is, quite literally, killing you, and us. Maybe it's time to start speaking up, for everyone's sake.

Your White Silence at Work: Regina's Story

As a very young woman in the early seventies, I started work at the Bell System at Mountain Bell, also known as AT&T, which at the time was the largest employer in the country outside of the US government. For Black people, it was a job that was right up there with working for the post office. I had to claw and fight my way into the business office rather than operator services, which is where they liked to place Black women. I spent several years as a first-level supervisor before being promoted to a staff position, which required a move to Denver.

The business office staff were the people responsible for developing practices and processes for all areas of work within business offices. Apart from one Latinx woman and me, the first-level staff managers were all white women. The second-level staff managers were predominantly white women with a man or two sprinkled in, and the directors were all white men, which was pretty typical for the seventies. The team I landed on was responsible for the entire Mountain Bell billing system. I found most people friendly, one or two absolutely wonderful to work with, and some who were less than kind.

One experience that left me perplexed was a group break. We were on the elevator returning to our floor, and I made a comment about myself as part of the group as a whole. I can't remember exactly what I said; however, I distinctly remember Mary Beth's response. Which was "Yeah, that's the problem." She wanted me to know that I was not like everyone else, that I was not part of the group, regardless of what I believed, that I was different because of my Black skin. My perplexity was driven by the fact that not one person, not the Latinx woman, not one person whom I called a friend, came to my defense. The people with whom I shared breaks, lunches, and lunchtime shopping were silent as a reaction to my humiliation and shame at a racist remark. And isn't that the point? You want us to suffer at the feet of your whiteness.

Fast-forward to 2015. My daughter is a counselor at our neighborhood high school. During one of our conversations, she mentioned that someone had started a mentoring program at the school and that I should volunteer. I signed up and tried to go to work. The founder of that program was a well-intentioned white woman whom I'll call Betty. The program was founded for kids eligible for free and reduced-price lunch who did not have a parent or guardian in the home who had graduated from college. Given the demographics of Denver City and County, that boiled down to mostly Black and brown kids. Having lived in a white body and raised two white kids, Betty frequently did and said things that I—as a Black woman, mother, and grandmother who had raised two Black children including a son, and was now doing my best to help with four grandchildren—found to be ignorant or wrong. Every single time I would voice my opinion, she would break down with the tried-and-true white woman complaint that I had hurt her feelings. No matter who you are, or how much I love you, I am not the one who will be held hostage by another person's feelings. I believe that as adults, we learn to, number one, understand that what we feel is a message from the universe to *us as individuals*. And, number two, we must learn to manage our feelings, just like we manage the rest of our lives. Sometimes that means doing the inner work.

Because these outbursts frequently happened at team meetings, I had no problem addressing them at team meetings, and that is when you could hear the crickets. If anything at all was said, it would not be relevant to what was going on, but rather to her feelings. I am not easily discouraged when it comes to advocating for Black and brown kids. Long story short, she resigned in a pile of hurt feelings, and I am still there trying to create opportunities for Black and brown kids.

CHAPTER FOUR

You See Oppression through a Gender Lens.

You Erase Your White Power.

You Are Colorblind.

You Are White Feminists.

A summary: You are expected to be perfect. To be perfect, you are required to be nice. To be nice, you must stay silent. You are often quietly seething about your perceived powerlessness. From this seething emerges a quest to try to reclaim your power from the primary oppressor: men.

This is your feminism.

You expect men to understand how they oppress you, while you remain unwilling to understand how you oppress Black, Indigenous, and brown people. How you oppress *us*—Black, Indigenous, and brown *women*.

You see oppression strictly through a gender lens. You understand how you are at a disadvantage as a result of misogyny, but refuse to recognize your white skin privilege.

Privilege is power.

By ignoring your white privilege, you ignore your white power.

When you ignore your white power, you uphold white supremacy.

This is white feminism.

White. Feminism. Is. White. Supremacy.

Let's recall that white cocoon we discussed in the preface. When you surround yourselves with white people, naturally, you white women will be the oppressed, compared with white men. Your white cocoon enables you to employ only a gender lens, erasing the individual and collective white power of your white cocoon.

Here's Lisa Bond again.

"I remember talking to a Black friend and co-worker several years back. She was telling me about her experience with sexual harassment and, in seeming solidarity, I told her a story about something that happened to me. And she said, 'No, Lisa. You don't get it. He didn't say these things to me because I am a woman. He said these things to me because I am a *Black* woman.' And that was the moment I recognized that the intersections of her identity were not the same as mine. That is the moment I realized that even in my womanhood, I still held power in my whiteness."

Black, Indigenous, and brown women sit at the intersection of race and gender, experiencing oppression that men of color and white women do not. This is called "intersectionality," a term coined in 1989 by Kimberlé Crenshaw, a Black woman professor of law. According to Professor Crenshaw, "Intersectionality is a lens through which you can see where power comes and collides, where it interlocks and intersects. It's not simply that there's a race problem here, a gender problem here, and a class or LBGTQ problem there. Many times that framework erases what happens to people who are subject to all of these things."*

So how does this apply to white women and colorblindness?

If all you see is white, you don't see color, right? Erasing your white power is a prerequisite to being colorblind, and colorblindness is a form of racism. If you don't see color, you don't see your white power, and if you don't see your white power, you don't see your racism. And if you don't see your racism, you cannot dismantle it. If you cannot dismantle it, you are actively supporting it.

White feminism 🤝 Colorblindness 🤝 Racism

One of the reasons white feminism is so insidious—and why white feminists might more often claim colorblindness (compared with white women who don't necessarily care about feminism)—is that white feminists like to think they live in a fantasy where every women is equally oppressed. You like to believe you are fighting for the rights and well-being of *all* women, and want to consider all women as equitable in that fight: it's so much simpler that way. Saying you are colorblind helps support your myth of equitability. You think you are being inclusive by saying you don't see color, but in erasing color, you erase your power and privilege over Black, Indigenous, and brown women. Without acknowledging this critical piece—and grappling with the racial oppression that Black, Indigenous, and brown women experience—white women lose the opportunity to organize effectively.

---

* "Kimberlé Crenshaw on Intersectionality, More Than Two Decades Later," Columbia Law School, June 8, 2017, https://www.law.columbia.edu/news /archive/kimberle-crenshaw-intersectionality-more-two-decades-later.

After Donald Trump won his election in November 2016, white women became activated. There was a flurry of excitement around political activism. Many of you who sat out the 2016 election started knitting pink pussy hats. Many of you who held your noses and voted for Hillary rolled up your sleeves and made posters by the dozens.

Girls Just Wanna Have Fun(damental) Rights

This Pussy Grabs Back

Nasty Women Rock

Roses Are Red, Violets Are Blue, I Love Smashing the Patriarchy with You

Throngs of you white ladies came together in the wake of Trump's victory. You were politically fired up, many of you perhaps for the first time in your lives. One of you called Saira on the phone. You had been given her contact information by a friend of a friend.

"I am interested in creating a website," you started. "For women. To fight back against this . . ." You lowered your voice. "Asshole."

"Okay," Saira said. "What exactly are you thinking?"

"Well, I hear you know media," you said. "And I'm thinking something *feminist*. Like a clearinghouse of all things woman. All things feminism. Like stories and links to websites and resources. But we should be able to opt out of things that we aren't interested in."

"Opt out of what?" Saira asked.

"Like, things that don't apply," you said. "You know, like Black Lives Matter."

Opt out of things we aren't interested in . . .

Things that don't apply . . .

Like Black Lives Matter . . .

This is white feminism.

Your feminism doesn't involve Black lives.

Your feminism is for white women.

Your feminism erases Black, Indigenous, and brown women.

Your feminism is colorblind, and it harms us, women of color.

Like many of you, this white woman no doubt spent a good chunk of 2020 talking about Black Lives Matter, maybe donating to BLM, likely wearing a BLM T-shirt or placing a BLM sign in the yard (until October, when Halloween decorations replaced it). A black square on Instagram for one day, maybe a week.

White feminists are nothing if not performative when it comes to antiracism work. This is what we call Performative Activism or Performative Allyship.

After George Floyd was assassinated by a white police officer on camera, so many of you were galvanized. Even those of you who said that Black Lives Matter wasn't one of your "issues" mere months earlier. Our inboxes were filled with your urgent requests. How can you help? What can you do? You wanted to do a Race2Dinner. You wanted to use your Instagram account to uplift the voices of Black women. You wanted to add links to Black-owned businesses on your websites. This behavior is what we call White Urgency.

More than three hundred of you sent us requests.

We responded to all of you.

Only one hundred twenty-five of you followed up. We spoke with all one hundred twenty-five.

Out of the one hundred twenty-five we spoke with, only three of you booked a Race2Dinner.

Your initial, urgent interest almost always gives way to your regularly scheduled programming of "being crazy busy" with kids or work or kids' schools or SoulCycle or a frantic combination of all of the above. If you were not in a white cocoon, but instead existed in community with actual BIWOC women, you would know that complaining about how busy *we* are all the time, in spite of also having children, jobs, and lives, is simply not a thing.

Your interest in amplifying Black, Indigenous, and brown women's voices on your social media came and went, a trend, like scrunchies; or like the time white actresses brought along women of color as their accessories to the Golden Globes. As for the woman who was keen to add Black-owned businesses to her business website? Well, she got "slammed at work" and abandoned the effort, but according to her Instagram, "slammed at work" meant a Caribbean vacation and multiple "self care weekends with my girls."

We get it. Massages in Aspen with your BFFs are warranted after all the work you put into posting a black box on Instagram. The work and cost it took for you to buy all those yard signs and antiracism books. You couldn't get back to us on that antiracism dinner you urgently wanted to plan last week because you ended up sending an email in support of the Latina woman running for school board and you were wiped out, recharging in the Berkshires.

You are tired, *exhausted* even.

You are women fighting the good fight. And you are tired.

Look, nobody is claiming you aren't tired or that you are not busy with jobs that overwork you, husbands who let you carry most of the domestic workload, divorces, ailing parents, deaths in the family, depression, anxiety, addiction, kids going through serious issues, debt, infertility. But if you are tired from all of this, imagine how tired *we* are. Chances are you haven't considered this at all, because either you don't see race, so you think we are all on the same playing field as women, or you don't see us as one of you at all (more on this below). The fact is, you don't care that we are tired. WAY MORE TIRED THAN YOU. Black, Indigenous, and brown women have been fighting this fight for centuries, way before you discovered systemic racism in the summer of 2020.

We. Are. EXHAUSTED.

Tired of racism. Tired of sexism. Tired of men, all of them. Additionally, we are tired of you. Finally, those of us women of color who speak up and out about racism publicly deal with the added fuckery of death threats.

Yes, death threats. So while you are feverishly getting lunches ready and kids off to school, know that we are doing the same *plus* hoping one of the many white folks who have threatened to commit bodily harm to us and our families is not hiding in a bush outside, ready to shoot our kids and grandkids.

Think about this the next time you feel exhausted by thinking about racism.

Here is white feminism in action:

1. You focus on gender.

2. You erase your white power.

3. You claim to be colorblind.

4. You uphold white supremacy.

5. Which harms Black, Indigenous, and brown women.

6. You act like you care about our issues when it behooves your image (kids in cages, George Floyd's assassination, anti-Asian violence).

7. Which is performative activism.

8. You *urgently* seek guidance from BIWOC, as you "listen and learn" and "want to do better."

9. You fail to follow through on the things we tell you to do as soon as the news cycle shifts.

10. Which means you have caused BIWOC to labor for you (in our case, returning emails, calls, texts) for free.

11. Your behavior is unchanged but you feel good due to your performance.

12. The performance has actually harmed us, as we are out of time and energy and resources fulfilling your requests, and you walk away with glory.

13. This is why many BIWOC prefer white women who do not pretend to care about their racism. Why a woman like Marjorie Taylor Greene can be less troubling than those of you who claim to be listening and learning. At least Greene isn't wasting our time.

At a dinner we had a few days after the terrorist attack on the US Capitol building on January 6, 2021 (note: most of the media does not refer to this as a terrorist attack, which is a function of white supremacy), we were talking about how the Nineteenth Amendment had effectively given only white women the right to vote, that Black and brown women had to wait for decades thereafter. A white woman angrily announced, "Well, first it's our turn. Your turn will come soon." We asked them to raise their hands if they were aware of the term "white feminism." Not one hand went up. Just because you are unaware of your racist pathologies does not mean they do not exist. Indeed your lack of awareness makes them that much more dangerous.

Then there is something astonishing that happens at almost every dinner. Well, astonishing for you, maybe. We are used to it.

You say a little bit about your own womanhood, something like "I worked for fifteen years while raising three children, and I learned about feminism from my mother when I was a girl. You know, she was a looney tunes feminist in the sixties." Later on, this same self-proclaimed feminist woman will get so defensive, so angry, that she will say something along the lines of "You all don't understand what it's like to be a woman."

You always reveal yourselves.

Regina will often smile and say, "You'll recall that Saira and I are both women. In addition to having Black and brown skin, we are also women."

After so many repetitions, we can laugh about the absurdity of it, but sit with those words. You white women think you are real women and we are . . . what, something else? You erase our gender oppression and fail to see how our racial identity intersects with our gender identity to create layers and layers of oppression. You will recall Professor Crenshaw's intersectionality from above.

So many of you laughed in disgust when Donald Trump proclaimed, "I don't have a racist bone in my body." You are so willing to see racism in others, but not yourselves.

You don't recognize your white feminism, its white supremacy, because you are constantly surrounded by other white women who parrot, reflect, and project whiteness. Your white feminism defaults to "feminism." Just like you are used to being simply *a woman*, rather than a white woman, so, too, are you used to thinking *your feminism* is the default, when in reality, it is absolutely racialized to our exclusion and detriment.

Your erasure of your white power not only hurts us, it hurts you. Let's go back to Trump, as he makes for an easy example on myriad fronts. Look at the numbers. Exit polls in 2016 show that 53 percent of you voted for him. Besides being a known racist, Trump was also a known rapist.

Your loyalty to whiteness trumps your loyalty to gender.

That's what led 53 percent of you to choose a white male rapist over Hillary, one of your own.

That's what led even more of you—a whopping 56 percent—to choose Trump again in 2020.

If your definition of feminism is *only* some version of gender equity and equality, then your white feminism isn't feminism at all, you see.

The truth is you choose whiteness over womanhood all day, every day.

This. Hurts. You. Too.

But that's the power of whiteness. It trumps all else, even your own well-being. Even the well-being of your daughters and granddaughters.

Until and unless your feminism includes a racial analysis, none of us will ever be free of white supremacy and patriarchy.

But don't take it from us, take it from a white woman.

"When it comes to feminism, we become the equivalent of white men," Lisa Bond says. "We are the center, we are the ones who know all, see all, do all. And anything that happens outside of our sphere doesn't actually matter. Take men out of the picture completely. What changes about these systems? Absolutely nothing, when it comes to race."

As we crafted this chapter, Lisa reminded us of a conversation we had with two white women who'd reached out wanting to potentially do a story on us for their local paper. It was at the beginning of the pandemic, in early 2020.

We will call them Judy and Jill.

They asked us to start with how we commence our dinners, so we did. When we noted that all white people are racist, they became enraged. We are used to this, as it happens often at our actual dinners.

So Saira tried to help explain it to them by saying, "I, too, have internalized white supremacy. What does that mean? It means I think white people are better than me. And as an Asian, I have been programmed to be anti-Black."

On cue, Judy sneers, "Regina, how do you like working with someone anti-Black?"

"We know everyone thinks they are better than us," Regina responds.

They are no longer sneering. They are pissed.

"I'm not anti-Black," they scream in unison.

"Yes, you are," we respond.

Audible hisses.

Lord help us.

"And by the way," Jill barks, "Asians aren't all anti-Black."

"Yes, we are, institutionally we are," Saira says.

"You have no way of knowing that," Jill asserts.

"I'm Asian. I absolutely know it."

"You don't get to talk for all Asians," Judy chimes in.

"Are you, a white woman, actually going to tell an Asian woman that she cannot speak to her community's experience with racism?" Regina asks.

"Just saying," Jill says.

"You're just saying what? That you, white women, know more about the anti-Blackness of the Asian community than a real-life Asian? Is that what you're just saying?"

"My God, you are angry. No wonder people hate you," Jill says flatly.

"Hate us?" Regina laughs. "You know what, let's move on. Let's discuss colorism and how you all—"

"Hold up," Jill interrupts Regina. "We have nothing to do with colorism. That started in Africa."

"Okay," Regina says. "So now you are going to whitesplain colorism to the Black woman?"

"You two are really one for the books," Saira says. "You are literally experts on everything, aren't you? Even us."

"I think we are done here," Regina says. "At least with our dinners, the white women are ostensibly there to learn something. You are here to teach us about us? Bye, Felicia."

We speak to lots of media. This was the first and only time we ended an interview early.

What did these women do?

They took to social media to mock us, to belittle us, to bring more white supremacist targeting and stalking into our feeds.

"In a nutshell, this is white feminism," Lisa says. "We actually are explaining to Black, Indigenous, and brown women their own issues. We are the bosses. The girl bosses. How can BIWOC want to be in community with us when we act like this?"

It's a great question, one that we ask ourselves often. But here's the deal: Imagine if you acknowledged your whiteness and could identify how it shows up in your lives. If you could do that (if you were *willing* to acknowledge what is plainly there), you could ostensibly begin minimizing the racialized harm you cause us. You could ostensibly stop voting for whiteness over gender, whiteness over all else. You could ostensibly start joining us in our crusade to overthrow white supremacy and the patriarchy.

You have power. You have white power. Until and unless you

recognize this, all you are doing is upholding violent systems of oppression that hurt us all.

Systems that hurt Regina. Hurt Saira. Hurt you.

The next time you feel that you are too crazy busy or exhausted to deal with antiracism work, remember this. What is the alternative? Do you want a "break"? Would you ever claim to be too exhausted to fight misogyny, to make the world more equitable for yourselves? For your kids? The break of which you often speak is actively upholding racism. Black, Indigenous, and brown women never get to take a break.

Your White Feminism in Action: Saira's Story

It was October 2017, about a year after Donald Trump was elected forty-fifth president, and nine months after a sea of white women pulled pink pussy hats over their heads and stormed cities all across America. I was one of them.

I was a few years into my involvement with a political action committee (PAC) that was run by women to get women elected to Congress and governorships. Or, I should say, run by white women to get white women elected.

There were about a hundred of us women in Denver. Everyone was white but me and one Black woman. Like I said, I was a white feminist—and TOKEN—for most of my life.

So I was not the least bit surprised, indeed I was honored, to be asked to deliver closing remarks at a fundraising luncheon for a United States senator, a white woman. The president of the PAC, a white woman whom we'll call Amy, sent a script that involved simply thanking the senator and alerting everyone about upcoming events. I was allowed to invite a guest, so I brought along my friend, a Black woman. There were roughly seventy guests there, all white women except for me and my friend. The only other people of color were the three Latino men caterers.

I listened to the opening remarks delivered by Amy. She bashed the racist and sexist Donald Trump. The white woman senator bashed the racist and sexist Donald Trump. The sea of white women in the audience hung on their every word, nodding, clapping, disgusted by Donald Trump's sexism and racism.

Then it was my turn to bash the racist and sexist Donald Trump, before basking in my tokenized glory, during which I'd tick off thank-yous and future agenda items. What an honor! My goodness, sharing a stage with a United States senator. How lucky was I!

As I stood there, next to Senator —— and before the dozens of white smiling faces, Amy staring, a director waiting for me to read her script, something snapped.

"I stand before you," I started, "as a brown woman imploring you to join me in this fight."

Amy's fake smile tilted. These weren't my lines.

"Look at you all. All white. White women."

Their collective grins started to look like Amy's. Wilted.

"A white senator."

The senator started shifting in her shoes.

"You all speak of the racism of Trump, and Lord knows Trump is a racist rapist."

The senator and guests calmed. Anti-Trump bashing, they knew.

"But my goodness, look around, everyone here is white except for me, my friend, and the people serving us food."

The white women spun around, noticing their white cocoon for the first time that afternoon, that day, that week, that month, that year, that lifetime.

"I hear a lot of white women"—the crowd cringed at the words *white women*—"talk about being an ally to women of color. But you have to reach across to us. We cannot make you do this. YOU have the power. We do not. It is incumbent upon YOU to do the work."

Blank stares.

"Just like it is incumbent upon MEN to do the work of dismantling sexism."

They calmed again, the gender lens providing comfort.

"White people, and you *all* are *white*, need to do the work of tearing down racism."

Silence. Total and complete silence. Amy in the back stood, arms crossed, completely still, any semblance of a grin having skipped town. Pure fury enveloped her face. An angry white mannequin.

"Thanks for coming," I remembered to say, "and thanks to Senator ——."

Senator —— awkwardly hugged me, and Amy unfolded her arms to clap, signaling an end to the white women's torture.

My friend and I left quickly, but not before the hostess caught me.

"I know someone who would really be interested in what you were saying," she said, her cheeks turning red with excitement.

"Great," I said, hoping she was about to say, "ME! ME!"

"Patricia Smith, I really need to introduce you to Patricia Smith."

"I know Patricia, thanks." We left.

My friend asked, "Who's Patricia?"

"Patricia is the only Black woman in the PAC and wasn't at the lunch today."

A month later, I went to Washington, DC, with the PAC. I'd caught wind of this event—and invited myself, much to Amy's chagrin. We met with another white woman senator who had her own PAC to help get women elected to office.

It was again a sea of white women, this time from all across the country, with a few of us women of color. The senator stood at a podium in the front of the hotel conference room and asked everyone to quickly go around and say why electing women to office was important and what inspired them to travel all the way to DC to support the cause.

White woman after white woman talked about gender and their daughters or their mothers or their nieces.

When I mentioned racial justice, many seemed embarrassed or surprised or both, as if the mention of racism didn't belong in their room.

About an hour later, Senator —— gleefully beamed her new home page up onto the screen. It was a selfie, with her in the front, leading a pack of giddy white women, about a dozen in all. Every single face was white.

I stood up and mentioned it.

At this point, a woman from the Arizona table turned and barked, "Not everything is about race."

Another said, "It's a freaking picture for Christ's sake."

Not a single woman there joined me in solidarity.

There's that white silence again.

After that, we broke for lunch. White woman after white woman came furtively to express their support.

You'll recognize this in yourselves. You won't publicly do the right thing but will send text messages, emails, or DMs to people of color in private. FYI: private support is not support. It makes YOU feel better but does nothing to stop the violence in real time. Make your support public or keep it to yourselves.

A staffer for Senator —— got my contact information to "keep the conversation going."

The conversation, however, had ended before it began. I never heard from any of them. Not even after repeated overtures on my part when I decided to run for Congress mere months later.

I learned shortly thereafter that the white women of the PAC had launched a whisper campaign about and against me. Words like "angry" and "divisive" were being batted around. A white woman new to Denver had asked me to have lunch and accidentally said, "Wow, you're not at all what I expected. The way they've been talking about you . . . you are super nice."

When pressed, she spilled the beans.

I promptly tendered my resignation to the founders of the PAC. Their responses were textbook white feminism.

One questioned what I "perceived." The other flat out didn't give a rat's ass and said a brisk goodbye.

> It is with a heavy heart that I am resigning from [PAC]. It doesn't feel like a safe space to me as a woman of color.
>
> There has been tone policing, gaslighting—and run-of-the-mill backstabbing—for which I have no tolerance. I have the utmost respect and admiration for the two of you and everything you both have accomplished. Know this decision has not been made lightly—and also know that neither of you are remotely to be blamed.

I'll be happy to share the details with you (although I'm sure you'll hear it from others). See e.g. backstabbing.

All the best,
Saira

Dear Saira,

I am very sorry you feel you must do this. I do want to have a call with all of us as soon as possible to understand what you have perceived

Thank you,

———

Hi Saira.

Sorry to hear that. We'll miss you. I wish you the best in your next endeavor.

———

Not long after, I wrote a piece for *HuffPost* about being a brown woman who was breaking up with the Democratic Party. It went viral, and I decided to move into action. So I ran for Congress against my super-liberal white woman representative who'd sat idly for two decades doing nothing and had the audacity to say, through one of her aides, "Civil rights are not one of my issues."

Shortly thereafter, I learned that the aforementioned PAC of white women had a stated goal of supporting women of color running for office in 2018. I would fit that description exactly. I called one of the founders, the one who had queried my perception of racism. She told me that she would not be supporting me because she was friends with the congresswoman. I noted that if I won, I'd be the FIRST WOMAN OF COLOR FROM COLORADO TO GO TO CONGRESS.

She told me that she didn't care for my tone, that honey attracted more flies than vinegar, and hung up.

Not one single member of the PAC supported my congressional run.

It is now 2022, and Colorado still has not elected a woman of color to Congress. These white feminists state goals of supporting Black, Indigenous, and brown women, only to do the exact opposite.

Your "listening and learning" is code for "knowing your racism and doing nothing to end it."

Not fighting to dismantle your racist ways *is* racism.

CHAPTER FIVE

Your White Entitlement.

Hopefully you can now see how white feminism is harmful. How in your quest to take your power back from men, you create new power structures, in which you take the place of—and act like—white men.

We refer to this as white woman entitlement. Referring to this particular behavior as *entitlement* is important. Why?

Language upholds white supremacy. The words "privilege" and "fragility" are so mild—so moderate, so proper, so subtle—when you consider what they are describing, the work these things do, the heavy lifting in upholding violence against people of color.

There is white supremacy in mundane, everyday expressions. Black cats, black magic, black sheep in the family. All bad. White lies, better than regular lies. Even "white trash." You don't say "Black trash" or "brown trash," ostensibly because it would be redundant in your white mind. When you say "white trash," what you are saying is trash is by default Black or brown. Pay attention to your words.

Just as problematic as what we say is what we don't say, namely our lack of vocabulary, its limitations. Without words to encapsulate your toxic white behavior, it often just goes POOF! It disappears—easier for you to claim it's a figment of our imaginations. Oftentimes, we'll just call your words and actions "white women nonsense," which diminishes their problematic nature; this language makes it sound silly, rather than dangerous. Or we'll throw everything into the catch-all box labeled "white privilege." Walking down the street, sitting in front of your house, going to work, shopping at the mall, without people wondering if you are dangerous, in a gang, an "illegal alien," a terrorist with explosives in your backpack, a carrier of the "China virus"—that's white privilege. Your mere existence is white privilege.

Yet the way you often act goes beyond white privilege. It's white privilege extra, white privilege on steroids, white privilege with a side of large fries.

It's white entitlement.

Regina's Story

"I recently started going door to door in my neighborhood asking neighbors if they would put a sign in their yard to support keeping a local city-owned golf course green rather than sell it for development. I went to every door in a large town house development on my block. When I got to the last house, a white woman on a moped stopped me and said, 'You can't put those on these properties, it's against the HOA.' I responded with 'I got permission from every homeowner before I put them in their yards.' She said, 'They don't make the rules, I'm on the HOA board.' To which I replied, 'Fine, they can take them down when you notify them.' She audibly huffed, to which I replied, 'Fine, you can take them down,' and I started to walk to the next block. She yelled, 'Hey, lady, I was nice to you!' I kept walking. Later that evening one of the neighbors stopped by to ask if I had removed the signs. I told him my story, to which he replied, 'A little power goes to people's heads' and that he thought that the city owned the lawn space.

"Saturday, I spotted said lady in her garage. I asked if she was the sign lady, and she replied yes. I stated that per my research, the property between the sidewalk and the curb belonged to the city and that I would be putting the signs back. She responded with 'You certainly are aggressive.'"

What's happening here with HOA Heather? Pretty simple. She is policing Regina, a Black woman, because she feels entitled to do so. First, why is she getting involved with Regina's action to begin with? Because she literally cannot stop herself. Heather is so used to being involved with—and controlling—everything that she is physically incapable of staying out of Regina's business. As we mentioned in the chapter on "white nice," this is you policing our behavior, behavior you deem to be not nice, without calling the actual police.

Second, HOA Heather announces her grand position as a board member because white people adore titles. You love setting yourselves apart—as better, with authority, in charge—by using titles and honorifics.

Third, when Regina does not respond with deference and obedience, HOA Heather lashes out with your favorite weapon, one that you should be able to spot a mile away—your niceness. Well, maybe your second-favorite weapon. You also treasure your white woman tears.

Fourth and finally, when Regina simply states her intention to return the signs after having done research, Heather delivers her final white woman blow by calling Regina, the Black woman, "aggressive."

Every single frame of these interactions, which in total lasted less than five minutes, contains a billion molecules of racism. Every frame is white privilege.

Every second is white woman entitlement.

As with all of our anecdotes, you may be shocked by Heather's behavior or grossed out or laughing at her. But don't. You have absolutely pulled an HOA Heather in your lifetime. More likely, you behave in this way regularly.

Saira's Story

"My son had a white friend over for a playdate. We will call him Ben. His mom texted me an hour before she was supposed to pick up Ben, saying she was having a crazy busy day and was held up at work and asking if I could drive him to lacrosse practice. I said sure, assuming it wasn't a FORTY-MINUTE drive during rush-hour weekday traffic. I was annoyed, but I said I'd do it, so I take a work call from the car and drive him there. We get to the field. Nobody is there. Ben calls his mom, and I'm stunned when he hangs up and says, 'Oh, she got it confused. Practice doesn't start for another half hour.' Full stop. Nothing about what I am supposed to do with this ten-year-old kid on an empty field. So I call her. Goes straight to voicemail. I get a text from her that says, 'I'm still on a work call. Will call shortly.' I am aghast. She just talked to her son but screened me. So I text back and say, 'I am just going to bring him home.' To which she responds, 'Okay.' I drive another twenty minutes to get him home, where a neighbor is out front waiting to drive him back to practice. It is another half hour before I get a text saying simply, 'Thanks.' That's the last I've heard from her and it's been four months.

"It occurred to me after that she was treating me like a baby-sitter. Asking to take her kid to practice, not answering my call, shooing me off by text because she was busy, not apologizing, and then not calling me again thereafter, like an employee who'd done a poor job. Her time, her work, her kid, and her life were more important than mine. So much more important that she rendered me an unpaid employee."

Like HOA Heather, Crazy Busy Caitlin is ENTITLED AF.

First, to think she can even ask Saira to drive her kid forty minutes away during a workday because *she* is too busy.

Second, not immediately fixing the situation when she realized what had happened. Why didn't she immediately call Saira to apologize and come up with a plan? Instead, she forced Saira to troubleshoot.

Third, she didn't even thank Saira for her effort. Of course, she said, "Thanks," but remember white woman nice. This "thanks" is not "Thank you. I appreciate you and your time." It's just the obligatory thank-you of a white woman being nice. How do we know? Because this thank-you was not accompanied by an apology. White woman nice doesn't require true repentance.

Fourth, her silence since the incident bizarrely reads as though somehow Saira was the offender in all of this.

This is classic white entitlement.

Other casual examples of your white woman entitlement:

1. Allowing your children to run wild on airplanes. A former white friend of Saira's relayed this story after a flight with her two-year-old son: "Al was stir-crazy, so I let him run up and down the aisles. But asshole Paul [her husband] grabbed my baby and forced him to sit, and when I got upset, he told me I was being ridiculous. Can you fucking believe he put a bunch of strangers before the needs of our child?"

2. Allowing your children to make a ruckus in public places. Kids will be kids, but it is your white kids who are allowed to act out with impunity. Not long ago, we were on a museum tour, and a young white couple was pushing a stroller with a toddler who kept screaming and throwing his sippy cup. It was extremely disruptive, yet his parents didn't say one word. Just kept handing the kid his cup back only to have it thrown again. The white woman tour guide finally had enough and asked the child to please stop screaming and throwing things, to which the white mother barked, "Don't you dare tell my kid what to do!" She and her husband stormed out. Everyone clapped.

3. Feeling entitled to every space. You throw fits at colleges and universities around the country that fund student groups for your Black, Indigenous, and brown peers. Groups that white students are not invited to join. This infuriates you. You have a hard time allowing your colleagues of color to form affinity groups at work without you. In some cases, you crash their meetings, even after being repeatedly told you are not welcome.

You are so used to having ownership over everything that being left out feels like death.

We see your white entitlement at all of our dinners, as early as the scheduling phase. Here is one salient example. It was just before the November 2020 election, and a group of white women in the New York City suburbs had been chewing on hosting a virtual dinner since George Floyd's murder. They were one of the few groups that actually followed through with us during your collective flurry of performative activism, which we described in the previous chapter. So good on them for that. Their white entitlement, however, showed up repeatedly during the scheduling. The number of "crazy busies" that flew around was staggering. There were work obligations, husbands, wives, kids, vacations. They were so sorry but . . . could we do this week? Yes. Oh drats, Martha's son is going off to college then. How about this one? Yes. Ugh, so annoying, Mary's husband is out of town and she has to hold down the fort. What about this one? Sure, yes. Polly got slammed at work and can't make it. Finally, there's a two-hour period that works in all of their schedules. This took *months* of planning, mind you. Then, about a week before our virtual dinner, someone in their friend group decides to throw a party and they all want to go. Can we shift the dinner to a few hours earlier? Yes, sure.

The scheduling of this dinner was one big exercise in white woman entitlement. Your time. Your schedules. Your families. Your jobs. Your lives. Not once did it occur to you that we, too, have schedules and families and lives and livelihoods. It does not occur to you because you are entitled to coming first, absolutely when it comes to us, Black and brown women, but also with one another.

And this is how your attempt to regain power from the patriarchy through entitlement hurts you too. By design, this requires you to compete with each other. You all have a pecking order among yourselves as to whose time and families and jobs and lives are more important than others'. Of course, the most perfect among you—which is determined by your white woman portfolio: money, marriage, niceness, kids, home, pedigree, thinness, beauty—always trounces the rest.

By the time each time and date was presented to us, you had

already had a mini Hunger Games among yourselves. Martha is the queen bee, so whatever she had going on clearly was more important than Meghan, who was more important than Alexis. All this violence among you was undoubtedly executed in silence or behind backs. Nothing was aired honestly and authentically. That wouldn't be *nice*. Only after exerting your entitlement over each other did you then collectively exert it over us, Black and brown women.

We are exhausted by your white entitlement.

Surely, you are too.

CHAPTER SIX

How Schools—and White Mothers— Uphold White Supremacy.

The kids are going to save us.

We hear some version of this sentiment all the time, along with these:

Once all the old people die off, things will be better.

Once all the racists are gone, it will all be fine.

Two sides of the same coin, the old are the problem, the youth are the solution—this theory is missing a key component of how all of this works. What keeps our society ticking. American schools are factories of white supremacy. Racism isn't an afterthought, a sideshow. It is, by design, the main event of every white institution.

When you say the kids will save us, you are not considering *what* they are learning at school, *who* is teaching them, and where that learning is being reinforced.

The what: a white supremacy curriculum.

The who: white teachers.

The where: at home, with you.

"You cannot fix the educational system—it is working. Its intent is to ensure white supremacy is longstanding. Whiteness is considered central and normal." These words are from Shana V. White, someone who knows, intimately, of what she speaks. White is a Black American middle school teacher in Georgia. "I am a survivor of the public school system, and I am making sure as many kids of color as possible can survive the public school system."

How does this system work?

It works like most everything in this country: white being the norm, the default, and everything else—everyone else—being the other.

"You are not going to hear about Black, Asian, Latinx woven throughout the year. They get a day, or a week, or a month. *Oh, we celebrate this month.* Do we even know the Indigenous origins of the land that our school is built on?" Shana V. White asks.

Some of you might be thinking, *That's just Georgia*—or *That's just how it is in the South.* This regional scapegoating is another way in which white supremacy persists, because white people in liberal enclaves feel immune to this ideology. But rest assured, every town, city, and state in this country is mired in white supremacy. From San Francisco to Boston, from Chicago to Austin. Even our nation's capital, where Kristin Mink, a Chinese American woman, taught for years in both private and public schools. Here is one of many anecdotes Mink shared with us about her experience.

"At the opening year staff meeting a couple of years ago, the whole middle school was meeting, and the principal was a white lady who was new. At the staff meeting she plays a video by Ali Michael, a white lady who specialized in antiracist education for educators. Ali says white people need to shut up and listen. At the end of the video, all the white people are so offended and do exactly what Ali just said not to do. Someone said, 'I can't be racist, I'm poor.' Another said she was offended because *she's* not racist. A bunch of white people complaining and talking about how they weren't racist, one person cried. The people of color just sat back and watched. None of us signed up for this. Just tell us where our classrooms are. The white principal did nothing. She let that shit happen. So all the white people were heard and all of us people of color were silenced. It was abusive. It felt like an attack on us people of color."

Myriam, a former teacher in Southern California who identifies as Chicanx, told us a story about a white woman colleague whose behavior was vile, sadistic, abusive, but not shocking. The perpetrator is the colleague. You identify the victims.

"One year I did not get my own classroom. Whoever did the room assignments did not factor me in. So I had to host my classroom in the office of a dean. We split the space. That dean used the office for half of the day. I often didn't have instructional time when she was in the room. There was a day we were together in our shared bungalow. She was on her side, I was on my side. She was engaged in discipline. She had a female student at her desk and she was berating the student, and the student didn't understand much because she didn't speak English. She spoke Spanish. And she was a new arrival to the US. The dean was berating her in English about an absence. And interrogating her, trying to extract information about the absence. The girl couldn't answer. She was nervous, and the more nervous you get, the less you can express yourself in a secondary language. At this point, the girl was speechless.

"I was witnessing this and I wanted to intervene but I was on special contract, meaning the district could fire me at will. I feared I'd be fired if I spoke up on the student's behalf. I was cringing in the corner as this tirade was happening. Then a lightbulb goes off in the dean's head because she remembers I am a Spanish speaker. She barks at me to translate. I don't want to do it. I am not legally required to do it. In fact, it's not legal for me to do it. So I go to the dean's desk and I take a seat. Now there is the dean, myself, and the student, and she orders me to give information to the student. I am to ask her who signed her absence excuse. I do. I ask her. She answers it's her godfather. In Latin American cultures, godparents are really significant family members. As much as blood family. I tell the dean that her godfather signed it. The dean says to tell the student that god family doesn't count as family. I modify what I tell the student. I tell her that a godfather is inadequate to sign for this. I don't want to tell her that her family is not her family. Then the dean says, 'I want to know why she was absent. It says she went to see a doctor. I want to know why.' So I ask the student. So the girl answers, 'I went to the doctor to get a pregnancy test,' and that she is pregnant. She had her godfather sign her absence because she is scared of being harmed by her biological parents if they learn she is pregnant. I only tell the dean parts of what the student tells me because I know she won't be sympathetic. The dean gets a smirk on her face and says, 'You tell this girl she needs to learn how to keep her legs closed.' I turn to the girl and I say, 'The dean and I are here to help you in any way we can. We will do anything in our power to help you.' I tell her the opposite of what the dean tells me to tell her. The girl is so grateful. The dean thinks I really showed the girl. I was sick to my stomach afterwards. I was abused in this situation. My language skills were abused by this white woman to sadistically humiliate a pregnant teenager. This kind of coercion is rampant in public schools."

This kind of coercion is rampant in public schools.

Every one of the educators of color we spoke to drove this

point home. The anecdotes they shared were just a few of *many*. Their personal experiences were common, not unusual. White violence inside of schools is a feature, not a bug. This is horrific, yes, but it should not shock you. Being shocked by white violence is white privilege. Black, Indigenous, and brown folks live with your white violence every day. It is not shocking to us.

If we have established that white supremacy courses through the veins of *all* white people, then why would we think educators are immune? They are not. It is irrational to expect otherwise. Don't take it from us. Here's Jessica Majerus, a white teacher at a public charter school in Oakland, California.

"Nearly ninety percent of teachers are white women. Not only is it a factory for white supremacy, it's a key place for white women to perpetuate white supremacy. Education is a transmission of values. When you have students in your classrooms, you are teaching them values. I know that lots of us like to say—I am in a lot of teacher Facebook groups—that we should just keep our opinions out of everything. That's ridiculous. Our values and the way we were raised just is a part of everything we do in the classroom from how we ask kids to line up, how we ask them to sit, how we arrange our classrooms. Our values and how we were raised in white supremacy is in all of those things."

Then there is the curriculum. Shana V. White says:

"The curriculum is Eurocentric and whitewashed so the perspectives kids are given are telling a story from a white male point of view. All other points of view aren't considered and are often omitted from textbooks and instructional practices. Most teachers are white, so they regurgitate the white curriculum. It starts as early as pre-K. As it gets close to fall and Indigenous Peoples' Day, it is called Columbus Day. Kids get dressed up as Natives and pilgrims. I said my son would not do that."

You may not notice this is happening, and may even reinforce it, because it seems normal to you; because your children are being taught the same things you were taught.

"It seems subtle in the beginning," explains White, "because most parents have experienced it, so they think it's normal. It takes someone from a marginalized group to say Thanksgiving is not commemorating a happy event. You centralize whiteness over all else."

A white supremacy curriculum is taught in most schools by overwhelmingly white women educators and then reinforced at home by you, who have been taught the same things by the same people. We will put that another way, as it is foundational.

Our kids read books that are filled with lies, books that erase the truth; our kids sit in classrooms where these lies are being fed to them, overwhelmingly by white women educators, and come home to discuss their days and get homework help from you, white parents, who learned the same lies from white women decades earlier.

Lie: Thanksgiving was a joyful celebration between white settlers and Indigenous people. Truth: white colonizers committed genocide of Indigenous people.

Lie: anti-Black racism ended with slavery.

Truth: anti-Black racism exists everywhere, from the school-to-prison pipeline to police brutality to whipping of Haitian migrants to grave economic disparity, and on and on.

Our education system is white supremacy on a loop.

So what is it like for Black, Indigenous, and brown children, being on the receiving end of this racialized violence in classrooms?

Regina's Story

"White teachers do horrible, shaming, traumatic things to children of color, especially Black children, each and every day.

"I will start with my own example from my early years. I think I was in first or second grade, and I needed to leave class to go to the toilet. My white teacher said no. The end result was that I wet my pants and had to spend the rest of the day wearing them. I don't remember if my teacher ever said that she was sorry, but what I do remember was being mercilessly taunted by white boys for the rest of the year.

"This is when I first acknowledged to myself, as a very young girl, that white teachers did not care about me.

"Fast-forward to sending my son to kindergarten. At that time schools were experimenting with 'open' classrooms, where several different teachers would have classes in a very large space where learning was supposed to take place. My son started kindergarten at the very same elementary school that I attended. I was a little excited about that because it was our neighborhood school. After the first grading period, I went in for a teacher conference. The teacher proceeded to tell me that my son (mind you, a kindergartner) did not have good social skills. I looked her right in the eye and said, 'The only social problem he has is you.' I proceeded to take him out of that school and move him to another school. How could anyone learn in that environment, especially a five-year-old?

"At his new school, his teacher was so excited when I asked her about his IQ score because she could not share that information with parents unless we specifically asked. His score was really high, and from that point on, I knew my son was gifted and I needed to engage differently for his sake.

"When my son was in sixth grade, we were living in a predominantly white community southeast of Denver that was still quite rural at that time. His teacher called me almost in tears because she could not get him to behave in class. I had a conversation with my son to try to understand why he was causing such grief for his teacher. His words to me were 'because she lets me.' From that point on, I understood that Black boys were the scapegoat for the entire education system. White women educators have zero expectations of Black children, and around sixth grade, Black boys get big; so then not only do their white women teachers have no academic expectations of them, they are actually afraid of them. And when you are afraid of your students, you let them do what they want.

"She would call me several times a week to tell me what he had done. I finally told her that she was going to have to figure it out, because he did not act like that at home, where he knew there would be consequences. Fast-forward, everything began to make a lot more sense when my son finally confessed that there was a white boy in his class who tormented him. He would call my son the N-word, hit him, and pinch him.

"I was livid! How could the teacher not know that this was happening? I set up an appointment and met the teacher at school. After hearing from me, she did her homework and found out from the boy's mother that his father was teaching him to hate and torment Black children.

"In high school, my son was not a serious student. What I know is that children live up to your expectations. If you expect nothing of them (as white teachers did), you will get nothing. My son was doing the bare minimum and getting passing grades. Then the day came when his school counselor called me to say, 'We have not seen test scores this high at this school in a very long time.' I had all the proof that I will ever need that white teachers are indifferent to the education of Black, Indigenous, and brown students. The children are not the problem, you are. You are the reason why Black, Indigenous, and brown children do not do well in public education. You get what you expect, which is nothing.

"Teachers had zero expectations for my son or any other Black child. I suspect that they thought similarly about any child who was not white. My beautiful, brilliant son had never been challenged throughout his school years. He told me himself that he had never had to work hard in school, until he got to law school. Thank God that he has his own gifts and me for a mother, or he could have been another statistic, to which white people would say, 'Well, you know how Black families are.' Because you are so entrenched in whiteness, you refuse to learn about and participate in other cultures besides your own.

"Many years later, I was helping my brother, a single father, raise his only son. I put T in an elementary school near my home that had a reputation for excellence. I visited T's second-grade classroom one morning and was very surprised by what I found. T was the only Black child in the class, and his desk was not with the other students' desks; it was right next to the teacher's desk. I questioned the teacher as to why that was.

"She went on to tell me a lengthy story about how she was so busy, and T was so talkative, that she needed to have him close by so that she could speak to him frequently. That conversation prompted me to volunteer to visit her classroom twice a week to help individual students with reading and math. Many of the students were not at grade level and desperately needed help catching up. One day the teacher asked who wanted to take some paperwork to the office. T and a little white girl both wanted the job. She pulled his shirt at the neck because she wanted to deliver the paperwork. In the process of pulling *her* shirt back, T accidentally scratched her.

"Do you know that the white principal actually tried to suspend T? Who in their right mind suspends a second grader for standing up for himself? When I spoke to her, she went on about how T left a mark on this little girl and how she could not let that go.

"I immediately called the area superintendent, had the suspension halted, and moved T to another school."

None of Regina's stories surprise Jessica Majerus, our white teacher from Oakland. Majerus admits to engaging in this very kind of thinking. That in spite of her best efforts otherwise, her whiteness still manages to show up at work.

"If I walk into a room and there are Black kids and they are loud and playing with each other, my first response is still—and I've quieted this response, I've learned to pause this response. But my first response is still, *Is everything okay in here? What needs to be fixed in here? Is a fight about to break out?* That's my first reaction. I have to say to myself, *Jessica, this is really normal kid behavior. They play with each other. You don't need to jump in.* That's my 'training'—to be afraid and fearful. That's anti-Blackness."

We heard a similar sentiment from Julie Cavanagh, a white principal at an elementary school in Brooklyn, New York.

"It is definitely a reality in public education and our country, the bigotry of low expectations.

"White kindergartners come in and they are seen as precocious or spirited or 'just so smart and so strong-willed' and that's where [their energy] is coming from. Whereas their Black peers are seen as 'their parents don't care' or 'they are coming from a broken household and this is trauma playing itself out and so they need an IEP (Individualized Education Plan).' Even in a school where you are deep in the equity and diversity work."

Among some of you, there is the notion that private schools are less racist than public schools. Something we hear a lot is "it's about class, not race" or "if you have money, you shouldn't complain about racism."

Money does not erase racism. But don't take it from us, listen to Rhea Rowan, a young Black woman who attended private school in Denver.

"My eighth-grade year was when everything wrong with the school came to light. My grade was already a pretty crazy class, but everything got worse when we went on a trip to Washington. It was the year of the 2016 election, Trump versus Clinton. My school was predominately white and, for the most part, everyone in that school—teachers, students—were Republican and openly pro-Trump. So, when we went to DC, everyone's racist tendencies came out. When we got on the bus, immediately, everyone was chanting, 'Trump 2016.' The group of minorities—me and a couple of Latina girls—just sitting there and not knowing what to do. Because most of the teachers were pro-Trump, they didn't do anything to stop it. It was just really uncomfortable. At that time, I was really good at saying, 'Whatever you believe is fine. But don't force it on others.' It was hard to accept, this guy was openly racist, and here was everyone celebrating him; even my teachers, who I thought would be educated enough to see past politics and acknowledge Trump was racist and misogynistic.

"When I talked to the Latina girls on scholarship, they were scared. Kids were telling them that their families were going to be deported and that all they would amount to were cleaning ladies and rapists. The kids were basically repeating everything that Trump was saying. It made me nervous for when Trump would have something negative [to say] about Black people. How would my peers treat me?

The whole trip turned out to be a negative experience if you were a minority. When we got back to school, the principal found out what happened and she held an assembly where she just cried for an hour. She was a white lady. The whole thing was pretty useless and no real action was taken. They tried to make us have talking circles where we would go around and say how we felt. This was useless. Everyone in the grade viewed it as a joke."

Let's parse this. This is a private school on a class trip. These children are more than 1,600 miles from home in the care of their teachers. They can't leave. They can't just go home. Essentially, they are trapped on buses, in hotels, at museums with their teachers, who are supposed to keep them safe. Instead, these teachers allowed their classmates to traumatize them, terrify them, make them think that their parents would be deported. This is a "fancy field trip," a culmination of middle school. It was supposed to be a treat. Their first time to DC. Instead: violence, fear, trauma. What does the white woman principal do when they are back? SHE CRIES.

Did money or class privilege protect Rhea and her classmates of color? And what happens to these Black, Indigenous, and brown students once they go to college? Here's Carmella Boykin, a biracial woman who identifies as African American and Italian. She's a recent graduate of Syracuse University, a private four-year institution in New York. We spoke with Carmella during her senior year.

"I've been part of the student-run TV station since freshman year. I was one of the only Black people at the station until this year.

"As a freshman, my first experience on air was when the student news director said to me, 'We have a racist incident on campus, you are our only Black student. Would you go on air? We need a voice of color.' They were really nice about it and I was glad for the opportunity, but it wasn't 'we have this opportunity and you are talented,' it was '. . . and you're also Black.'

"My junior year, same thing, another story. There were reports of fraternities on campus being racist, saying the N-word to students of color. The school didn't take any public action. So, a group formed called #NotAgainSU. They had sit-ins and protested in a few buildings on campus.

"Our station had a brainstorming session to talk about what angles reporters could cover. One of the white reporters at the station said, 'My friends and I aren't really impacted by this, so we can talk about how this isn't impacting parts of campus.' I was shocked she made this campus issue about herself. The idea could work, but not if only white voices are included in the story. We're covering an issue affecting primarily Black people. That was one of the few instances I felt truly alone at the station. Sitting at the anchor desk looking around the studio crammed with at least thirty students, I was the only Black person in the room and one of a few people of color. No one else spoke up.

"This was the first time I ever raised my voice at the station. I said in complete disbelief, 'There are racist incidents happening around campus and you want to talk about how this doesn't impact YOU. You are a white woman. You'll never even *begin* to understand this until you talk to Black people and other people of color.' That's where the problem is. Detracting from people of color and bringing it back to a white narrative.

"There are very different worlds happening all across the campus, and the worlds are different for white people and people of color."

Boykin hits the nail on the head: *The worlds are different for white people and people of color.*

In every facet of this country—public, private, north, south, east, west—there is a different reality for white people than there is for people of color.

And that reality affects our schools.

So the next time you talk about how the kids are going to save us, think about who's teaching the kids, what they are learning, and who's reinforcing all of it at home.

CHAPTER SEVEN

"Microaggressions" and How You Kill Us at Work.

We are going to be honest: it's not easy working with you.

White women constantly throw us under the bus. You silence us, steal our ideas, inflict "microaggression" after "microaggression." We put that word in quotes because there is nothing micro about the hate you give in boardrooms, operating rooms, newsrooms, classrooms, kitchens, bars, theaters, stadiums, Hollywood, Broadway, Silicon Valley, the Republican Party, the Democratic Party, party planning, and every other workspace.

Hearing this likely hurts your feelings. After all, aren't we in solidarity, struggling against the dudes who run our industries? But the very same things you complain about men doing to you, you do to us. And men do the same—if not worse—to us, so we are dealing with *layers* of nonsense.

Recall the white woman from chapter 2 who called us to consult with her about her start-up company. The one who asked for our opinion on her DEI efforts. The one who told us that if we were nicer and if we changed our tone, perhaps white people would be inclined to be less racist.

This same white woman has undoubtedly experienced, at the hands of men, the kind of violence she inflicted on us. Perhaps even in a similar context. Perhaps a male colleague, likely a superior, asks her to join a conversation about sexism in their workplace. She comes to the table in good faith. Surrounded by a group of men, she explains how one can't "fix" the sexism problem at the company just by hiring a handful of women. They must actually commit to eradicating sexism from their operation, culturally and institutionally. Anything less would be cosmetic, and could incite more violence towards women at the company. In such a case, it's very likely she'd be called unreasonable, asked to reconsider her position. She may even be called into a separate meeting with human resources, told to change her tone. She may be ghosted, demoted, even pushed out. Perhaps axed from the industry altogether.

White women often mimic the oppression of white men, asserting their institutional power over those below them in the American hierarchy of racism and sexism. That means us: Black, Indigenous, and brown women.

In other words, you, white women, learn from your bosses, white men, how to shit on those beneath you in the pecking order: us.

You. Know. What. You. Are. Doing. Because. It's. Done. To. You.

Sometimes it is hard to see how one's own behavior is problematic, so we provide examples in the form of real-life experiences from women of color. These women work in different fields, yet all of their experiences—as women of color who work with white women—echo each other's.

As you read these anecdotes, consider how they would feel if they were about how men treat you, white women, at work.

You Assume You Are More Competent Than Us

The biggest thing as a therapist is that the majority of white women that I encounter automatically assume I'm incompetent. **They immediately tell me how I should do my job, give me advice.** "Oh, I just want to give you some advice. I'm doing you a favor." It's a constant fight to get them to see me as an equal. Part of our profession is referring clients to each other. Once you provide a referral, you typically have no further contact regarding that person. In one case, a white female therapist makes a referral to me and proceeds to call me every other week. She wants to know what's happening. At one point she calls me, and I realize I am trying to prove myself, to prove to her that I'm a good clinician—I'm competent. She calls with "I want to check in." She states she has had communication with my client and starts to tell me, "Hey, I'm not sure if you have the right type of training, but if you do this, it might be helpful." I'm in shock. She proceeds to tell me how to do my job. We have no other relationship outside of this referral—she's a peer who is assuming the role of clinical supervisor with me, telling me which interventions I should use and how I should work with this client. We are the same age and both fully licensed. Regardless of that, this is completely unsolicited and inappropriate. I ultimately have to completely cut off communication with her. While this case was extreme, it was not an anomaly. I also believe she would never treat a white peer this way.

—**Marisol Solarte-Erlacher, Colombian and Mexican American, psychotherapist**

You Belittle, Diminish, and Silence Us

My experience working with white women has been identical and replicated from office to office. It is the act of intentional erasure of your presence while you are being invited into the space or the "table"—what Lama Rod Owens refers to as "white supremacist grace."* In this "white supremacist grace," BIPOC bodies are physically allowed into white spaces but expected to sit quietly in the corner in gratitude, unacknowledged and also reminded of our place in this act of erasure. This term describes my experience with white women in public health perfectly. Public health as a sector is dominated by white women (nationwide data demonstrates this). **And so as a Latina woman who has infiltrated this white woman space, I often wonder if white women only know to interact with me as they would a house cleaner or custodial staff (a sector dominated by WOC in the US).** Like muscle memory, I wonder if their only experience interacting with me as a Latina, or a person inhabiting a Latina body, is from

* This term can be found in the book *Radical Dharma: Talking Race, Love, and Liberation*, in the chapter titled "Remembering in Seven Movements," in case you need the proper citation.

this idea of a simultaneously invisible yet service-oriented body. That's the only way they know how to behave. And so I sit in meetings, in discussions, where pleasantries are exchanged among white women and not with me. I'm asked to close the door or to take notes, but not to share my opinion. When I forcefully get my word in, I am interrupted before I finish my thought by a white woman who needs to share what she thinks I wanted to say—like if the words coming out of my mouth necessitated white savior interpretation to the group. And hilariously, white women always seem to explain my thoughts back to me A-LIT-TLE-LOU-DER-AND-SLOW-ER . . . to make sure I understand. To make sure I remember my place. And I remember. I remember I am my grandmother Jesusita's daughter who always said, "Let there be one fool and not two" (que sea un loco y no dos).

—**Mariana del Hierro, Latina, public health**

You Steal from Us

It's obvious how many times a day white women steal ideas and work from Black and brown women. The interesting part is they claim to be helping us, when in truth they are making a profit or gaining power for themselves. I learned recently that white progressives going after funding will name-drop Black and brown people that they are associated with to raise the funding, but they do not intend to give any of that funding to those organizations. So most of these organizations don't even know they are being named. White people will give funding to white people as long as they name-drop a Black organization enough. While our names are being used, we don't know what's happening and we aren't granted any of it. We are starved from the funding while what we do is used as leverage for funding. I only learned this after the fact as I was struggling to keep Digital Sistas going. I helped a friend get a job with one of these organizations—I coached her through applying for it. I tried to get her to negotiate better, I was also a reference for her, and she got the job. When she goes into the job and reads over the grant that got her hired, she sees my name and my organization. That means the only reason I know about my name and organization in a grant is that someone who is a friend read the grant and told me. These white women write grants with my name and my organization for them and their funding, but never talk to me and never offer a sliver of their grant money. I don't know them. Nobody has come to me to offer me anything. If this woman didn't know me, she obviously wouldn't have told me. This is a practice. They consider this normal. They know my work. They know what I'm doing. **They are using me while still in public they act like I'm not important and not doing anything. But privately they are using me and stealing from me for their gain.** My ideas, my work, my experience. Yes. It's a practice.

—**Shireen Mitchell, African American, founder of Digital Sisters/as and Stop Online Violence Against Women Inc.**

You Talk a Big Game about Diversity while Inflicting Violence

My favorite instance of dealing with white women being toxic was the time I tried to insert "antiracism"—literally, that language—into our City Council Rules of Procedure document. It's about our council's intent, how we engage with each other and conduct our business. I really wanted to insert antiracism language in there. I was trying to call out how my council colleagues were weaponizing the section on rules of decorum, which is steeped in white supremacy and patriarchy, and I thought using the term "antiracism" would help us collectively agree to be more conscious of how we perpetuate oppression under the guise of "professionalism." The white women on the council lost their entire fucking minds. I'm literally trying to *teach* them about white fragility and how it plays out and how it influences our work. One said, "Antiracism isn't 'measurable' . . . so it doesn't belong in there." The other one claimed, "We don't know enough about this." It was an entire meltdown—textbook white fragility on *full* display after I just taught them what white fragility is and how it perpetuates oppression. **We talk about equity all the time, it's exhausting. But when it comes down to decision-making, and how equity plays into our decisions, it flies over their heads.** It is their very reality, one of being white, that doesn't allow them to see another reality. Because they are in a position of power, there is no real reason for them to see anything through a different lens.

—**Candi CdeBaca, Indigenous and Mexican American, Denver City Council**

You Question Our Every Move

When I'm doing major donor calls, which is nonprofit parlance for face-to-face meetings where you are courting someone to be your highest donor, **I find that with white women—there are more and more questions. This constant "pick pick pick, I'm going to pick at you."** White women lack the awareness to ask, "Am I exhibiting behavior that is counter to the cause that I'm trying to support?" The constant questions come across as them not trusting me as a Black woman, not trusting the leadership of a Black woman. Specifically, because my predecessor was a white man who had the position for seventeen years, and by his own admission, he was not a good fundraiser. We lacked cohesive programming for seventeen years. And yet, people still funded the work at that time. They ultimately supported my white predecessor's leadership. Having doubled our revenue in a relatively small period of time, I'm still questioned as if I don't know what I'm doing. That is the pick pick pick that drives me crazy. I inherited an organization that ran a deficit every year. We haven't had this problem under my leadership. When I'm speaking to a donor and they are questioning me, it is offensive and it feels racist. I can only surmise that their issue is me, a Black woman.

There was this donor, a white woman, who made a $100K pledge over the course of ten years. Two years after I took the job, she canceled the pledge. She did this after the 2016 election, after 53 percent of white women voted for Trump, saying she wanted to put her money into "other things." She'd been a donor for over thirty years. I took that personally. The two-year mark into my tenure. I was still creating the infrastructure. She'd been supporting our organization for so many years prior to my arrival, under white male leadership, it did feel personal. There is a lot of that.

—**Shay Stewart-Bouley, African American, executive director of Community Change Inc. and founder of Black Girl In Maine**

You Expect Us to Do the Most for the Least

There are a lot of white men and women involved in political organizing. In Miami, we were organizing health care workers, mainly home health assistants, nurses, janitors, building service workers. Nearly all of the people we were organizing were Haitian and Cuban immigrants, yet the leadership team of the labor union in Florida consisted only of white people from the Northeast. One of the people I directly reported to was a white woman in her forties who had the attitude that "if you don't work eighty hours a week, you're worthless." There was no space for my mental health issues—issues I've had my whole life. I would never be able to work eighty hours a week. I burned out. I would get guilt-tripped. **That is the biggest thing white women have done to me: guilt-tripping me for saying I can't do everything, for having to say no.** I'm not allowed to say no. Every time I said no, I was told I had to remove myself. I can't work these hours, but it was an ultimatum. I was told that if I couldn't work eighty hours a week, I would have to leave. Bear in mind I was making around

$35K a year and expected to work eighty hours a week and was burned for not being able to do that because of my mental health issues.

—**Nina Baliga, South Asian American, former labor organizer**

You Erase Us and Deny Our Oppression

When I have a problem that is about race in the workplace, my colleagues assume that I'm not that kind of Black person. I can't be George Floyd or Sandra Bland because the degrees erase everything Black about me. The racist stuff they do is based on *their* version of my Blackness. They only see a shallow end of a Black person, rather than a full spectrum of the Black experience. This is why diversity can't save us. They aren't seeing my entire experience. They don't see my fear of running into a racist antagonist on the subway on my way to work. By the time I get to the office, and we are talking about diversity, they are treating us all as equals, and equality is not equity. Anytime I remind anyone that I'm from the streets, anytime I bring the street into academia, I am the one who has to bear the burden of the discomfort of white folks. Silence. Awkwardness. Or open hostility. People objecting to the idea that I'm oppressed because I hold a PhD.

—**Dr. Tamara Lee, African American, professor**

You Mispronounce Our Names. Repeatedly.

I am a survivor of narcissistic whiteness. As a little four-
year-old Mexican immigrant, I arrived in Denver,
Colorado, with my father in 1979. We lived in a small
apartment with his sister, her husband, and their three
children for just under a year. He worked and saved up
money to send for my mother, who had also managed to
cross the Rio Grande with us the year before but stayed in
El Paso, Texas, awaiting the impending birth of my little
brother. He was born right before my father and I left for
our trek north to Denver. She named him Edgar. Shaking
my damn head . . . My parents had made an agreement that
my father would name all the daughters, and my mother
would name the sons they had. My father had hoped he
would be able to name all his children with Indigenous
Nahuatl (the language of the Azteca) names. My mother
went on to have another son, and she named him
Christian. I am still shaking my damn head. As a year or
so went by, I learned some English and managed to help my
parents order McDonald's for all of us as a five-year-old.
I then arrive to kindergarten after the school year had
started. The white female teacher calls my name by
saying, "Ex-oh-cheetill, would you please stand in front of
the class to tell them your name and how to pronounce it?"
My body heat rushed to my face as the classroom burst
into laughter, and I felt terribly embarrassed as I walked
to the front of the classroom. I say my name—Sō-cheethil
or Sō-chee. "What does it mean?" she says. I explain that
it means flower. I sit down. She continued to pronounce
my name as "Saw-chee" for the rest of the year with no
regard for how I felt about being forced to stand with

shame and humiliation as the children laughed throughout.

Thus began, what I had to accept at the age of five, the norm of whiteness that requires people of color to accept white women's sense of self-importance, constant attention to their needs, and their privilege in this society. For children of color, it is the stark reality of having to learn in school that of a societal hierarchy and racial structure and where you land in it. Forty years later and most white women I work and engage with continue either to hesitate to say my name at all, which allows them to not call upon me or to pass me over for paid work that I am qualified for, or to mispronounce my name without asking for the proper pronunciation and assuming they know it all, including how to pronounce Indigenous names. The lack of empathy, entitlement, and white privilege that white women have held and continue to hold in these United States of America is the narcissistic whiteness that I have had to learn to endure and survive from the age of four. **The integrity, the value, and rights of women of color with names foreign to the likes of Sharon, Karen, and Lauren do not matter, because if they did, it would mean that white women could no longer take advantage and exploit us to self-aggrandize.** From not being called for job interviews to not accepting my clients' real estate offers to buy a home has impacted my sense of self, well-being, and livelihood. I have been forced to get creative with my interpersonal and communication skills so that I can maneuver through the norms of whiteness. For example, I have found a way to be assertive toward white women, without their perceived aggression of women of color, to acquire paid work to survive narcissistic whiteness.

—**Xóchitl Gaytán, Mexicana/Indigenous Latina, small business owner and entrepreneur**

You Cry Violent Tears

There are so many instances where white women have burned me, but the one that immediately comes to mind is when I was working in the social services sphere. I was a teacher in a treatment facility, and a fellow teacher—a white woman—made some uncomfortable and racist remarks to the kids we were working with. It was everyday racism. I created a space in my classroom where my kids were allowed and encouraged to speak out. My kids unknowingly picked up on the power dynamic and knew they couldn't fight back against her, and they told me about it. I scheduled some space and time with her. I told her this wasn't acceptable and why what she said was wrong and she owes me and the kids an apology. It was a very calm, professional way in which I spoke to her. She then scheduled a meeting with our supervisor, another white woman, in which she claimed that I was mean, that I was combative, and that I had an attitude and that she felt unsafe because of what I was saying. She never addressed that she transgressed against the kids and what she said and did. **This was an actual opportunity to fix her relationship with the kids, and instead she immediately** leaned into her white privilege and tattled on me. In the meeting, she cried. And that shit shifted the meeting. I knew then that I wasn't being listened to. When she turned on the waterworks, I looked like the villain, especially because I remained stoic and professional. So she used her tears in a position of power. Her racism was glossed over and never addressed. I wasn't professionally reprimanded. There wasn't a write-up. But I did get unofficially reprimanded. I was told to dim my personality and that I was too intimidating. She used her white woman tears to create a hostile work environment for me.

—LadySpeech Sankofa, Black American,
former social worker

You Blame Us for Your Bad Behavior

I was the director of programs at a nonprofit focusing on education. I was the leader of my department, managing multiple teams, with only the executive director above me. I had to hire someone to be my direct subordinate to manage specific programs, and my team and I chose a white woman candidate. We will call her Anna. The understanding was that she was the most qualified, at least on paper, so I hired her, and the problems started immediately.

Anna, who was one of three direct reports and the only white woman on my team, was combative with me from the beginning. She would ignore my directives and do things her own way without explanation, walk away while I was talking to her, and ignore requests for one-on-one meetings. **I mentioned to my executive director, "Karen," who was new and also a white woman, that Anna was toxic to my team and undermining my position. Karen's response was to send ME to management training. So I had to take time out of my weekends to travel hours to a management coach in order to learn how to manage this disrespectful person.**

Management training did not help. Anna was as intransigent as ever, while my ED specifically asked me not to push her too hard.

Aside from being disrespectful, Anna was also entitled and a liar. As a new parent with limited daycare options, I would work eight to four, then rush out to pick up my kid from daycare, and then work an additional half hour when I got home. Anna insisted on modifying her own schedule in response, supposedly from ten to six. I would leave at four, and she would sneak out soon after. This happened for almost a year before I found out, because despite Anna's toxic behavior, I wanted to trust my team. I mentioned this to Karen, again to indifference. In Karen's eyes, Anna could do no wrong, and I was too hard on her, despite treating her with kid gloves and the fact that I was the supervisor.

Another person on my team was "Tran," an Asian woman who was and is the best worker I know: highly credentialed and a dedicated, creative, and kind worker and manager. Every meeting with Karen, for a full year before I left this job, included me praising this woman's work ethic. When I had to leave this job to move to another state kind of suddenly, I gave three weeks' notice and recommended Tran as the person who could seamlessly transition into my position. I wouldn't have had to train her, and she wanted the job too. Instead of hiring the Asian woman, Karen approached Anna, the white subordinate who had spent the previous two years antagonizing me and actively undermining me, and asked her to take over my position. Then she offered Anna $10,000 more in salary than what I'd been making after four years with the organization. When Karen told me this, and asked me to train Anna, I refused. Anna had spent the previous two years acting like she had absolutely no need for my guidance or expertise—I was not about to spend my last few weeks at a job I otherwise had loved dealing with someone so toxic. As a result, I was asked to leave the job two weeks earlier than anticipated.

—**Cynthia P., multiracial Afro-Latina, nonprofit sector**

You Say Racist Things in Front of Us—and behind Our Backs

There was this white woman who is a teacher. Kids complained that she was incredibly boring and the story checked out—whenever I walked by her classroom, half the class would be asleep, and the only times she was animated were performative anti-Trump tirades. One day one of her students complained to me that this teacher does not like Mexicans. The kid told me that she teases Mexican students about having lice in their hair and will tell them they can't take off their hats because lice might get on the desks.

I was livid when I heard that because that was the stereotype that was used to give Mexicans chemical baths along the US-Mexican border in the early twentieth century. This student also told me about how she said she wouldn't let her own kids play with Mexicans because she didn't want them to get lice. So I was really pissed. About a week after I heard those stories, I was in a teacher's classroom during noninstructional time and I was getting coffee. **The anti-Mexican teacher was there at the same time as me and was having a conversation with another teacher. Since the conversation was moving in a racialized direction, I started to get nervous. I had a sense that someone was going to say something disgusting.** To head them off, I turned around and interrupted them and casually mentioned that I was Mexican. The anti-Mexican teacher got a disturbed expression—one that combined shock and anger. She insisted, "Well, I didn't know!" as if I was withholding information from her.

I said, "Well, I am. I am Mexican." She said, "Well, I thought you were Indian!" She said it in an accusatory tone, as though I had tricked her into thinking I was Indian.

She found me intelligent and clean. To her, Mexicans aren't intelligent and clean, so she found an appropriate racialized category to put me in. She made me Asian.

It fucks with your stress level. As a minoritized teacher, I didn't have the same stress levels as my white colleagues. I am Chicana and I am queer, so my stress levels are different.

—Myriam, Chicanx, teacher

You Think You Are Better Than Us, Even if You Work for Us

Jenny was a young—in her twenties—skinny, white woman from rural Pennsylvania, and this woman worked for me and yet had absolutely no respect for me as a boss. This is when I had my restaurant—Anthony Bourdain had come in before (the restaurant had been featured on his CNN show *Parts Unknown* in the past year), I had already received one James Beard nomination for Best Chef of the West. And yet I was told by one of my servers that Jenny once lamented to him that she was wasting her time and talents working for me. Let's be clear. Jenny was not so gifted in the kitchen. First and foremost, here I am, I was about forty-two, so I'm about twenty years older, and I worked about double the amount of hours in a given week, yet this young woman had to constantly complain how tired she was. I am trying to imagine my twenty-four-year-old self complaining to the chef. There is a problem in our industry for the lack of care for our bodies and our emotions. This wasn't that. This was just regular twentysomething wah wah wah. My chef de cuisine was a Black woman. Single mom of two gorgeous boys, and a badass in the kitchen. Sometimes the two of us were having a discussion about the team and upcoming service. Jenny needed to tell me later on that she thought it was so rude and disrespectful that the two of us were talking about her in front of her, and that she could tell. We weren't saying her name. We were talking about the staff and getting ready for service. She could tell we were talking about her, and that was so disrespectful. I was like, we are your bosses. We weren't saying anything rude or offensive or personal. It was work stuff. It was operational work stuff.

To her, she saw a Black and a brown woman gossiping about her rather than "these are the chefs who I work under, who have so much more skill than me, and they are discussing the team from an operational perspective." I had a talk with her and a young Black man who had been working for me for a few years, since he was out of high school. I had to redirect him sometimes. So I sat him and Jenny down together, and this young man was like, "I hear what you're saying, Chef, and I'm going to work on it," and this woman basically sat there, this twenty-four-year-old woman who had just graduated from culinary school sat there, and told me I was wrong. She was so defensive that I told them they needed to pick up the pace and work on their skill level. It was all operational stuff, and I told them, "There are positions up the chain that I'd love one of you to work towards." The young man said, "Yes, yes," and I had to dismiss him to go back to work because she was getting combative instead of listening to my feedback to improve. She looked at me and said, "I have what it takes to become a great chef one day." She basically wanted this position the next level up without having to prove the capability of doing the job, and she could barely handle the role she was in, which is why I sat them down. Her stance was she should have an even higher position. There was constant devaluing when she worked for me. I offered to introduce her to chefs for her next job. When I said that, she couldn't believe I knew famous chefs. Because what I looked like and the ethnicity of the food didn't translate to that in her eyes.

—**Preeti Mistry, South Asian American, chef, author, podcaster, and activist**

You Speak over and for Us.
Quite Frankly, You Treat Us like Shit.

Saira's Story

Several years ago, I was at a meeting with a white woman colleague. It was the two of us and about a dozen folks from another company. We were there to make a pitch. The head of their team, a white woman, turned to us and said, "Can you please introduce and tell us about yourselves." My colleague went into great detail about her life, her work experience, and then it was my turn . . . only it wasn't in her mind. Just as I was about to open my mouth, she starts speaking *for* me. Saira grew up in Virginia, she went to UVA, then on to law school, and on and on. I was stunned. This same woman used to bitch and moan about sexist men, and what she did to me was like having a dude order for a woman at a restaurant. She took away my agency, she dictated my narrative, and she showed everyone in that room who was boss. I was rendered speechless the rest of the meeting. This is merely one of hundreds of cuts I've had inflicted upon me throughout my career. So, too, has Regina, who spent three decades in corporate America, slowly climbing the ranks into a C-suite position.

Regina's Story

Whatever our educational, social, or business achievements, you never think that we are as bright, educated, high-status, or worthy of all that you have.

In 1977, I got an acting promotion to assistant staff manager at Mountain Bell, one of the original telecom companies, which required me to drive to Denver from Colorado Springs. There were two other women from Denver, who were also acting, as we were in the midst of a big system upgrade. I was a small-town girl working in the big city Monday through Friday. I didn't know that we were all being observed and considered for *one* permanent position. My white woman colleague—we'll call her Karen because why not?—*did* know. One day, the manager called me into her office and offered me the position. I accepted. I was excited to tell my peers the good news.

But the reaction I got from Karen was so racist and hurtful that I was taken aback. "The only reason that you got the job was because they needed a diversity hire," she said. Not only that, she proceeded to tell the manager that I had "bragged" about getting the job. I got raked over the coals because a jealous white woman, who was not qualified for my position, weaponized her whiteness against me.

I fought those white women. I just never realized as a young person how radically different I was. A very young woman who spoke her mind.

When I was first hired, they were looking to hire women into operator services, which was a 24-7 job, so that's where they put the Black women. Well, I told the hiring manager, a white woman, "I don't want to be an operator." She said, *That's all we have.* I said, *Well, I'll wait.* I didn't want to work weekends, nights, holidays. A couple of months later, I got a call, and they had a job in the business office. At that time the business office was almost all white, college-educated women. There was me and maybe two other Black women out of about one hundred to one hundred fifty people. Eight to five, five days a week.

I had a white woman boss say to me, "Regina, you run your mouth all the time. The only thing that saves you is ninety-nine percent of the time you know what you're talking about." I was very talented, I knew my job, I did it very well. So if I knew what I was talking about, how was that just "running my mouth"? What she was saying is, *You don't have the right to question things. You are just to do as you are told.*

My first supervisor, Geri, a white woman, would use every excuse to return work to me to do over. We had an organizer on each desk, and she was always bringing stuff back to *me* saying I was doing stuff incorrectly according to the BOP, which was short for Business Office Practice. So you know what I did? I became the expert on the BOP. I knew what the BOP said. I knew it inside and out. She'd come to my desk and say I wasn't doing things right, and I could then say, *I know what the BOP says.* She left me alone after that. I had to be better, or else she would keep picking on me.

Very few of you go out of your way to hire, mentor, or promote Black, Indigenous, and brown women, which is exactly what you must do; if anything is ever going to change, you must. You are too busy sharpening your knives against each other. You never see us as fitting in, as being competent, as having a spark in us that needs to be nourished. You don't see that we are smart, we are talented, and we have good ideas. It's always about what we don't do "right" (read: "like you") and it's never-ending.

Twenty-seven-plus years. That's how long I spent at AT&T and US West Communications, climbing the ladder despite the anti-Blackness, racism, and misogyny, and retiring in 1998. Over and over again, you challenged me to keep my cool, to move through or around your bullshit. Even though all of your opportunities were created on the backs of Black people, including me.

My last promotion before retiring from the company was to executive director, reporting directly to the general manager and executive VP of Large Business & Government Sales & Service, who reported directly to the CEO. I was told to pick any office on the twelfth floor that I wanted. As I moved my boxes into the corner office of my choice, with windows overlooking the Coors baseball stadium, a white woman who reported to one of my new peers challenged me by saying, "Who told you that you could have that office? Ken has someone in mind for that office." How it was resolved, I don't know, but I called my boss and let him know what had happened. I never heard another word.

A life well lived is about doing the inner work and uplifting those who have needs that go unanswered. Black people *know* that you believe we are lazy, that we don't work hard, that we *like* being poor and depending on public assistance, that we have babies to get welfare. Even with proof throughout US history that all systems have been, and still are, designed to keep us from living the lives that you have. When and if we do achieve the American dream, time and time again, it is burned out, bombed out, and destroyed by white hate and jealousy.

Back to "microaggressions."

Definition of "microaggression": a statement, action, or incident regarded as an instance of indirect, subtle, or unintentional discrimination against members of a marginalized group such as a racial or ethnic minority.

Having read all of the above examples of your hate in the workplace, would you call any of them "micro"? Would you say your actions are indirect, subtle, or unintentional?

The impact is direct, overt, and damaging.

Behavior matters. Stop being racist. Language matters. Stop diminishing your racist acts by calling them "micro."

You can do this.

We know you can do better because we, ourselves, have witnessed it.

We recently did a Race2Dinner with the white women leaders of an international company. The president of the company—we will call her Jenna—is a white woman who had made some incendiary (read: racist) comments on Saira's Facebook a few years earlier. Jenna did something that we rarely observe: she swallowed her pride and reached out to us to organize a digital Race2Dinner with the white women on her leadership team. After all the participants introduced themselves, Jenna did something even more rare. She publicly acknowledged the harm she had caused Saira. She apologized. She did so in the presence of nearly a dozen white women who work for her.

Jenna was honest. She told the truth. She did better.

And guess what? Her employees followed her lead. Each and every one of them acknowledged how their own racism appears in their daily lives. If their boss could acknowledge her racism, so could they.

One by one, they spoke of clinging to racial stereotypes, seeing their Black, Indigenous, and brown women colleagues as lesser, as divisive, as angry. They spoke of their silence in the face of overt racism. They spoke of their need to be liked at all costs, and no matter *whom* it costs. It goes down as one of the best Race2Dinner events we have had. Have those women all continued the work? Probably not. But we know that at least a handful have, as we continue to be in conversation with them.

That is progress.

January 9, 2021

Dear white women:

It's been three days since white nationalists stormed the US Capitol in an attempt to overthrow the government and steal an election at the behest of their leader, US president Donald Trump.

A Nazi leading Nazis. A terrorist attack. Although many of you aren't calling it that. Had those wielding guns and grenades been Black, Indigenous, or brown, named Mohammed, chanting Allah, you'd feel differently.

We know some of the villains of the day. We saw them on TV. But the other villains, the ones who didn't storm the Capitol, who were appalled, shocked, horrified—they are getting less airtime.

They are you.

White women. In many cases, politically liberal or moderate, even leftist. In other cases, conservative. You live all over the country. Big cities, small towns. You are Democrats, Republicans, Independents, Socialists, Green Party, Antifa, or Apolitical with a capital A. You are doctors, lawyers, baristas, janitors, teachers, elected officials, rich, poor, gay, straight.

The one thing you have in common is the most powerful characteristic of all: whiteness.

Last night, January 8, 2021, two days after the coup, nearly a year into the deadly pandemic, we did something stupid. We agreed to attend a dinner with nine of you in person, at a hotel conference room. We risked our lives and those of our families to subject ourselves to your racism for two hours.

Shame on us.

But really, shame on you.

Your behavior was abhorrent. Not surprising, of course, but abhorrent nevertheless. You were nine white women in the same organization. Highly successful corporate, academic, and nonprofit leaders. It was two hours of raw, overt racism, sustained by just about every participant during the entire dinner. The takeaway: you not only haven't learned anything from the Great Antiracism Summer of 2020, you have gotten worse. You have stepped all the way into your whiteness, not even bothering to disguise your disdain for us.

There was promise early on, when we asked you each to tell us about a racist thing you'd done or said recently. There were stories of playing white savior and swimming in white guilt, an anecdote about painting Black folks as a monolith, the paradigmatic tale of tokenizing a person of color employee. There was real promise that you were all willing and able to engage in some self-reflection, but that came to a halt pretty quickly.

One of you was a white woman who claimed Indigenous heritage. An Elizabeth Warren Indigenous woman. Later on, when it was pointed out that your group was all white—meaning there were no women of color among your leadership ranks—you pointed to the fake Indigenous woman as your diversity before saying, "Shouldn't you just be happy that there is progress here, that there are nine of us women who have broken through the all-male ranks of this organization?" Regina asked why *we*, as women of color, should be happy, when it's not progress for us. The white woman huffed and puffed and told us that change takes time and our turn would come eventually. Saira asked her if she knew what white feminism was. She didn't. Saira explained that it was viewing everything strictly through the lens of gender, without a racial analysis, and seeing the white woman's oppression at the hands of white men as the sum of all oppression. She rolled her eyes.

There was a tech CEO who told us that she refused to accept that white women had more privilege and power than men of color because men of color had an easier time getting money in the tech world than white women. We asked her if she had stats on that.

She did not. We then asked her if she understood that she would never get killed or beaten up or harassed, her kids wouldn't be threatened, because of the color of her skin. She crossed her arms.

A posse of white women at the other end of the table whispered among themselves, rolled their eyes in our direction, and kept muttering that they didn't agree. A woman who was an immigrant from Germany did not like being called white because she was German. The other women backed her up. We asked the entire room if they knew the difference between race and ethnicity. Not a single one did, yet they each took on the role of the expert in the room when they spoke, claiming more knowledge than us.

They were unmoved by our personal tales of racism. They flat-out didn't believe us, didn't care, or both.

There was one white woman who seemed to somewhat get it. She pushed back against some of the other women's racist statements, but in the end, she didn't like it when we said that they had much in common with the rioters at the Capitol. Sure, we assume they would never participate in a violent Nazi coup attempt, but they all shared toxic whiteness.

She steadfastly rejected this.

We left soon thereafter.

Until and unless you all appreciate how whiteness is the evil, we get nowhere. We will have more white riots (terrorist attacks). We will have more white nationalists elected to local, state, and federal offices. We will have more poverty and violence, and less education, housing, and health care.

We will continue to sink into a pit of despair.

You have the power to change this.

Please use it.

With love and hope,

Regina + Saira

P.S. Some of you might be rolling your eyes at this very moment. A few early readers of this manuscript—white women—had the reaction of "come on, we are not as bad as the January 6 rioters." Here's what we said to them—and what we say to you. Why do you need to distance yourselves from them? What is the compulsion to be *less bad*? Racism, whiteness, white supremacy culture is ALL BAD. Do you think quiet Germans, the ones who did not personally murder a Jewish person, were less bad than Nazis? One group made the other group possible. Please interrogate your need—and your desire—to be less bad. Instead, perhaps expect more from yourselves. Stop focusing on being perceived as less bad and strive more to do better.

CHAPTER EIGHT

Every Time You Say Love Trumps Hate, You Are Enabling Hate to Flourish.

Love trumps hate.
Love wins.
I choose love.
Focus on love.
We need to come together.
Unity.
I choose to focus on that which unites, not that which divides.
Be positive.
Don't be so negative.
Stop being so doom and gloom.
Maybe you are reading into that.
Maybe that wasn't about racism.
That happens to me and I'm white.
Lighten up.
Take a joke.
Heart emojis.
I don't see color, I just see love.
Namaste.

All of this is extremely toxic.

It's a mix of spiritual bypassing, gaslighting, colorblindness, and toxic positivity with a heavy dash of cultural appropriation. Let's ground ourselves with definitions.

1. Spiritual Bypassing: a series of moves rooted in "spirituality" that white people make in order to avoid discussing the brutal realities of white supremacy.

Examples:

"We have to stop dwelling on the past and move forward."

"We are all part of the human race."

"Manifest your way to happiness."

Rather than "I understand our violent white supremacist past and present and how we, white people, are responsible for it and benefit from it. Until and unless we white people dismantle white supremacy, I understand how there can be no unity."

But nope, you drop a bunch of platitudes about love, light, and healing instead.

Common spiritual bypassers: white yoga instructors, white healers, white wellness instructors, white spiritual leaders, white self-help experts, white self-care specialists, white "gurus," white people who use the terms "spirit animal" and "my tribe," white life coaches.

See it in action:

At every dinner, without exception, at least one white woman spiritually bypasses us. An example: We talk about how white supremacy is destroying all of humanity and the earth. We will mention gun violence and climate catastrophe—and how every single white person, indeed whiteness, is culpable. At this juncture, a white woman will say something like "well, I choose love" or "I prefer to focus on the good." In December 2021, we did a Race2Dinner Zoom with two dozen white educators and parents in Denver. About forty-five minutes in, a white mother raised her hand and said, "I hear you about being in the fight against racism, but I want my son to have fun and light and happiness. I refuse to subject him to this heaviness all the time."

At the time of publication of this book, choosing love and focusing on fun hasn't ended racism.

2. Gaslighting: a type of psychological manipulation in which one person or group will work to plant seeds of doubt to make another person or group question their own memory, reality, or sanity.

Examples:

"Are you *sure* they said that?"

"Come on, that's an exaggeration."

"That happens to me all the time and I'm white."

"That wasn't racist."

Any and all expressions of shock over personal stories of racism.

Rather than "I see you, I hear you, I believe you."

Common gaslighters: white people.

See it in action:

Ana is Mexican American, and her boss, Rebecca, is white. They work in an office, Ana as Rebecca's assistant. Ana's common duties at work are creating expense reports, scheduling meetings, and doing research for new business opportunities. One day, somebody spills something very gross and messy in the office kitchen sink. Rebecca asks Ana to clean it up—even though manual labor is not in her job description and she's wearing a nice blazer and blouse that could get stained; not to mention the fact that she's in the middle of a time-sensitive data-entry project and really doesn't have time to clean the kitchen. Frustrated, Ana turns to her colleague—Jessica, who is white—one cube over and says, "I don't want to seem like I'm not a team player . . . but I just have this feeling that she asked me because I'm Latina, and I don't know if she would have asked me to do this if I were white." Jessica becomes visibly uncomfortable, and keeps her eyes on her computer screen instead of looking at Ana. "I don't know," Jessica says. "I don't really see the problem. You're her assistant. I don't think you should make it into, like, a racial thing."

Now, Ana has to clean the sink, getting her nice clothes dirty, and she's also worried that Jessica seems to think she's being overly sensitive, and maybe even a little crazy. As she's scrubbing, Rebecca walks by, with Jessica and some other junior colleagues who are also white. It looks like they are on their way to have lunch together.

3. **Toxic Positivity:** a form of psychological manipulation that relies on inadequate and excessive overgeneralizations of happiness despite a person's emotional pain, experiences, or difficult situations. It works to invalidate, diminish, and minimize the very real and lived experiences of the targeted person or group. It is a form of spiritual bypassing.

Examples:

"The best is yet to come."

"Look on the bright side."

"If I can do it, so can you!"

"Everything happens for a reason."

"Look at how FAR we've come."

"It could be worse."

"Can't we all just get along?!"

"Just LOVE everyone."

Common purveyors of toxic positivity: white people.

See it in action:

Adrienne is in twelfth grade and she is Black. She is the only Black student in her civil rights seminar at a predominantly white school. Adrienne feels awkward, as the teacher seems to be presenting racism in America as a before-and-after binary: before the civil rights movement of the 1960s, America was a very racist place, and afterward, things were better. Even though she's only seventeen, Adrienne knows this isn't true. Everybody assumes she got into a top-tier college—where she will be attending in the fall—on a sports scholarship, but she's a really excellent student and could go to the college of her choice. When she and her friends play "celebrity look-alike," they always tell her she looks like Rihanna, but she looks, literally, nothing like Rihanna.

Adrienne stays after class one day to start a dialogue with her teacher about what she sees as an oversimplification of racism in this country. Her teacher tells her that, historically, we have come so far and made enormous strides. She says that the objective of this class is not to make the white students feel bad about the state of the world today, but to teach them about some of the incredible people who helped change the world in the 1960s. Later that week, Adrienne's mother gets a phone call from the class dean. The dean tells Adrienne's mother that some of her teachers are concerned that she has a "negative" or "combative" attitude in the classroom, and that, at this school, they work hard to foster a positive and constructive learning environment.

4. Colorblindness: the abusive misinterpretation of Dr. Martin Luther King's words, "I have a dream that my four little children . . . will not be judged by the color of their skin but by the content of their character," wherein white America replaces race consciousness with obtuse know-nothingism. This stance allows the "colorblind" person to ignore the very real harm of systemic inequities, while also pretending they do not have any personal biases.

In sum: if you don't see our Black and brown color, it makes it super easy for you not to see your very real white racism.

Common colorblind folks: white people.

See it in action:

Person of color to white person: "What you just said is really racist."

White person: "That's impossible. I don't see color. It's literally impossible for me to be racist."

The end.

5. Cultural Appropriation: when a colonizing culture steals or adopts objects, elements, customs, and the like from another culture without recognition or consent, especially specific to elements that have been "racialized" or deemed undesirable by the colonizing culture when used in proper context by the original culture.

Common cultural appropriators: white people.

Shirin is Iranian American and she is a chef and a food writer. She is used to white people thinking the food she makes is weird. In elementary school, her white friends would stare at the lunches her Iranian-born mother would make for her. For years, working her way up the ladder at New York restaurants and online food magazines, she has tried to get her superiors excited about recipes that are inflected with her heritage, but she's always been told they're "too ethnic" or "too weird." At the cooking website she works at now, in her first week, she pitched a piece on rosewater cookies for the

Iranian New Year, but her boss said it was a little too niche. A couple of years later, another staffer—a white woman named Jenna who is very friendly with the boss—writes and publishes a piece on tahdig, but she calls it "Persian-inspired crispy rice." The article becomes extremely popular, perhaps because the boss promoted it heavily on the website's social channels—and Jenna is promoted to editor.

There is *always* ample use of *all* of the above at each of our dinners.

Always. All. Each of our dinners.

At all of our dinners, we see white women behaving badly. We see you deflecting your racism, denying racism altogether, bright-siding racism. It's like clockwork.

It's this clockwork piece that seems to get lost on you. Like everything else, you think your platitudes are somehow novel, that we haven't heard them before, that we don't hear them every single day. That they are helpful, clever, even ingenious, rather than harmful, common, and intellectually vacant.

When we lift the veil on these particular moves, the ones you think are rarefied and brilliant, you get more confused and coy than you normally are. Your pretending not to know about your toxic behavior reaches new heights. Now you know that your pretending not to know has a name. GASLIGHTING.

So to make it super simple for you to grasp, let's lay out a scenario that might feel familiar.

You are in a work meeting with a group of dudes. They are talking over you, talking for you, taking credit for your work. You are irate, upset beyond belief. You have had it. You take it up with your boss after the meeting. After all, he was there, bearing witness and actively causing harm. You explain how the sexism at work has become unbearable to you, that this meeting was the perfect example. What does he say?

"Nobody said anything sexist in that meeting, at least that I heard."

You tell him that it wasn't so much the things that were said, but the way the meeting was conducted, and the general lack of respect for your contributions. You are getting even more angry about the fact that he's not being receptive to your complaint.

"You sound really angry right now. Let's talk when you're less worked up."

You tell him that, yes, you are angry, but that your anger is valid, and your anger should not negate the fact that the men in the meeting were out of line.

"Our success in this department depends on us being able to work as a team. I'm hearing a real you-versus-them mentality in what you're saying. I wish you would try to be more collaborative and cooperative, try to see them as your teammates."

You tell him it would be easier to feel like a part of the team if you were treated equitably, given the same respect and consideration as your male counterparts.

"Whoa, whoa, if you're insinuating that you are treated differently here, that's ridiculous. I don't see you as our 'female team member.' All I see is a bunch of hardworking go-getters.

"Frankly, I'm offended that you even think I'd be capable of treating you differently. I have daughters. I hired you, didn't I?"

You each have experienced a version of this at the hands of a man (or many men), be it a partner, spouse, co-worker, family member, friend, or neighbor. At work. At home. At school. At your kids' school. At a party. At a cookout. At the mall. On the street. On a plane, a bus, a subway.

You all know what this feels like. His responses are a denial of your experience. A denial of his violence. An erasure of your experience. An erasure of his violence.

Deny what he's done. Deny how it has caused you harm. Erase the entire thing. Expunge the record. That is how sexism endures and persists generation after generation.

Boys, as children, learn to engage in this sexism early and often. Girls, as children, learn to internalize this sexism.

This occurs in exactly the same way that you, as children, learn to engage in your own brand of racism. As adults, you teach your children the same.

It is early October when we sit down for a Race2Dinner in Denver. The home is Halloween ready, with little pumpkins adorning the table and paper skeletons dancing on doors. The mood is festive, the wine flowing.

We start our conversation over a plate of steaming noodles, marinara, and salad.

Liza, the hostess, mentions that her seven-year-old daughter wants to be Pocahontas for Halloween and that she knows it's "probably not politically correct" but she doesn't want to "crush" her "tiny spirit."

"That's straightforward cultural appropriation," Saira says. "I'm not sure why you'd use the term 'not politically correct.' The actual term is 'cultural appropriation.'"

"And it's extremely harmful," Regina adds.

"Harmful? *Please*," says Stacey, a woman with red hair and a jean jacket, shaking her head in opposition. "See, *this* is what makes me sad. The anger, the divisiveness. Liza's daughter is in *first grade*. Can't we just let her be a kid for God's sake."

"A kid at the expense of Indigenous people? A kid who is able to put a costume on—for fun, when an entire people were victims of genocide? Indigenous people aren't able to wear and take off their identities at will, the way Liza's daughter can with a costume," Saira says.

"Why do you think you can take everything for yourselves?" Regina asks. "White people came here, stole the land from Indigenous people. Killed off Indigenous people, and now you think your little kids can play dress-up. It's sick."

"Wow, you don't have to be so rude. We can talk about this in a nice way," Stacey says, crossing her denimed arms, the common choreography of white women resting their racist cases.

"Wait!" Liza interrupts. "Everyone, this is exactly why we are here. To listen to Regina and Saira. Not argue with them. I'm sorry I even brought up the Halloween costume," she says, hanging her head in white woman victimhood.

"Don't be sorry," Regina says. "Like you said, this is why we are here. I just think it's amazing you all think you and your kids can dress up in anything, at any time, without pushback. You are so used to doing anything you want without criticism."

"She is a *child*," Stacey barks.

"You realize that there are Indigenous *children*, don't you?" Saira responds.

"I really wish we could all just get along," Jennifer, one seat next to Stacey, pipes up. "This makes me so sad."

"Yeah, it's just Halloween. I kinda think you're taking this a bit too seriously," Meg says, a skeleton's head peeking up behind her head. "It's supposed to be a fun holiday."

"Making light of genocide is fun for you?" Regina asks.

This is a very unpopular statement, and just about all the white ladies come to Meg's defense, as if Regina has mortally wounded her.

That's not what she meant and you know it.

You need to apologize to her.

That's a nasty thing to say.

You culturally appropriate (Pocahontas costume).

You are called out (in this case, by us).

You deny (Stacey).

You diminish (Stacey and Liza).

You spiritually bypass (Stacey and Jennifer).

You gaslight and torch with toxic positivity (Meg).

Your feelings are hurt, so you gang up against the truth tellers (the white women there, against us).

And normally you get away with it. Just like the men in your lives when it comes to sexism. At our dinners, during the two hours when your butts are in chairs in a room with us, you do not get away with it. But that's just two hours out of an entire lifetime. What happens when you leave and go back out into the world?

We happen to know that Liza's daughter did not dress up as Pocahontas that Halloween (she went as a shark), but how many kids and you, their parents, *do* celebrate Halloween by dressing as Indigenous people or Mexican people or even by wearing Blackface?

According to Regina, the whole point of Blackface is to de-mean Black people. "The term 'Blackface' specifically refers to the makeup worn during minstrel shows, which existed for the pur-pose of lampooning Black people, and perpetuating racist stereo-types about them, for entertainment. We are the butts of your jokes. For enslaved Africans, English was a second language. White people still minimize, mock, and distrust people for whom English is a second language. Mexicans, Black people, Indians, anyone with a foreign accent. Yet most white Americans don't even speak a second language. STOP with the Blackface, STOP minimizing people who speak English as a second language, STOP pretending you can't understand what they are saying when they speak with an accent. In short, stop being a butt crack."

Regina's advice, namely to stop being a butt crack, seems

easier said than done considering how often you continue to dress in Blackface and brownface on Halloween. And when you do, you claim that you didn't know it was racist or xenophobic.

Playing dumb is also gaslighting, by the way. So yes, even the subtitle of this book acknowledges your gaslighting: Everything *You Already Know* about Your Own Racism (but pretend not to . . .).

A few weeks after the Denver dinner described above, Saira was walking through town with her son and ran into a few kids he'd gone to school with years before. They were dressed up for Halloween. One wore a Broncos jersey. Another had brownish makeup on his face and was wearing a backpack. Saira's son asked what he was.

"A terrorist," he responded proudly.

He was in the third grade, and his white mom smiled and waved from half a block away. She was chatting with a crew of other white moms.

According to Saira, her son looked confused and upset, so they left immediately. He asked about the kid's costume, so Saira told him the truth. She told him it was Islamophobic, xenophobic, racist, and flat-out hateful. She posted about it on social media. And right on time, a liberal white woman from New York City came into her mentions, berating her for "criminalizing a little boy." When Saira asked the white woman how her own little boy, the brown one, was made to feel, she blocked her.

The white woman blocked Saira for asking her to consider the feelings of a brown child, her brown child.

Do better, white women. Questioning you, holding you accountable, or God forbid, critiquing your words, is not criminalizing you. Yet it feels this way to you. Saira's mere pushback on social media cut at this white woman's sense of perfection and goodness. It was easier to block Saira altogether than grapple with her question.

You all are the first to police us. Yet when we ask simple questions, you quickly pull down the shades, unwilling and unable to see the truth of yourselves.

This need for things to be rosy at all times is also an example of toxic positivity, something it behooves us to delve into further, as your toxic positivity has picked up steam side by side with the (equally toxic) self-help and self-care movements (of white women).

Toxic positivity means forcing a glass-half-full attitude in every situation, including when police repeatedly murder Black people; white men shoot up grocery stores, schools, and movie theaters; our government separates children from their parents at the border; COVID decimates our population; and climate catastrophe unfolds.

No matter what, you are conditioned to remain positive, because you're not supposed to inconvenience the people around you with negative realities; you're not supposed to seem bitter or shrill; you are conditioned to stay upbeat, to think about the good, to focus on being happy.

Doing so requires you to deny, deflect, erase the oppression that is eating away at marginalized populations. According to you, white women, our pain is a downer, a bummer, the opposite of happy, the opposite of fun. Our pain is pessimistic.

Our pain is harshing your mellow.

At one of our Zoom dinners, shortly before the November 2020 election, one of the three dinners that came out of the more than three hundred requests for them, the following went down.

Loads of chatter about Donald Trump, the Orange Cheeto, the monster, and how he was toast. We agreed, we hoped desperately that Joe Biden would win. We said it was absolutely necessary that Donald Trump was removed from power, but that Biden becoming president was not sufficient to end the racism in our country. After all, racism was around long before Trump, and as we have noted before, racism is likely responsible for Trump becoming president in the first place.

A symphony of toxic positivity erupts.

"Oh, come on, don't be so negative," one of the thin, blond women says, squinting through the bright sun into the computer camera.

"Yeah, ladies, haven't we had a tough enough four years that we can actually consider a bit of happiness here?" another chimes in.

"I, for one, am just psyched to be able to sleep at night without worrying what that psycho will tweet next," a third says. "And once Biden is there, he'll make sure COVID is gone, and maybe we can even get back to doing things we love, like going on vacation and having brunch."

The thin blonde perks up. "Totally, brunch. God, I miss brunch. Can't we just enjoy the *prospect* of brunch?"

"You can imagine that even before Donald Trump, Black people couldn't enjoy brunch in peace. You'll remember that white people kill us for sitting, standing, sleeping, breathing," Regina states matter-of-factly.

A collective sigh.

"I *know*," one of them says in a fashion that indicates just the opposite, "but can't you just look forward to a little respite? A little light at the end of the tunnel."

"That's just it," Saira says, "Regina is telling you that it has never been safe for Black people in this country. What is the light you're referring to?"

"I just choose hope and joy. We're all entitled to happiness."

For four years, liberal white women lived in a heightened state of anxiety and discomfort because of the climate that

Donald Trump created. The everyday trauma of having a rapist in the Oval Office—and to have to constantly hear his voice and see his face on the news—was triggering to many of us. For the first time, perhaps in your entire lives, you white women had trouble sleeping and trouble focusing, just knowing that someone was in power who was actively trying to hurt you. Trumpism has clearly bled into our daily lives as little kids are "grabbing pussies" on the playground and reality is dubbed "fake news."

"What I am trying to tell you," Regina says, "is your hope and joy and happiness don't save Black people. That for Black people, it has always felt this way. We aren't just worried about tweets. We have always worried about getting killed for just going to work. You're worried about kids saying jokes on the playground. We have to worry about that and our kids getting killed on the playground. Shot for holding toy guns like Tamir Rice. I will bet some of you don't even know who Tamir Rice is. Go google his name. These past few years, you have experienced one tiny itty-bitty fraction of the anxiety that we experience every day. To tell us we should just sit back, relax, and enjoy the prospect of Joe Biden is your white privilege talking. It's your white supremacy talking."

Silence.

A silent sea of blinking white eyes zooms onto our computer screen, reminiscent of fake ghosts in a Halloween cartoon. Only these are real white women in real life.

Don't do this, white women. Stop denying. Stop deflecting. Stop erasing. Stop brightsiding everything. The only people served by brightsiding racism are you white folks. You commit the harm and then expect us to see the good in it.

Toxic positivity not only calls for erasure of our reality, but is truly evil for the way in which it implies that we, Black, Indigenous, and brown women, are somehow bad—lesser or weaker—because we refuse to deny or erase our own pain. You see this positivity as a virtue and, in relief, our refusal to be positive reads as a defect. You want us to see pleasure in the pain that you inflict.

We are downers for not smiling and saying please and thank you while you kill us.

It is sadistic.

The bright side, being positive, *love*—none of this stops police from killing Black people, or stops our government from separating and caging Black and brown children, doesn't protect Asians from being beaten on the street, and doesn't bring back the thousands of Indigenous women and girls who have gone missing. Being positive doesn't stop your white children from traumatizing our Black, Indigenous, and brown children at school.

Uplifting, inspirational memes don't end racism.

Thoughts and prayers don't end racism.

Wishing away racism doesn't end racism.

Your going back to brunch doesn't end racism.

We know that your heroines tell you just the opposite. You know, the ones whose books you eat up, classes you take, memes you share, Instagram accounts you simply cannot live without. The girl bosses. Boss babes. Healers. Yoga instructors. Peloton instructors. Pure Barre instructors. Lovers of all things namaste and Spiritual Gangster. Instagram influencers. Green juice makers. Sourdough bakers.

These titans of the white American wellness world are wreaking havoc on us—and you.

We turn again to our Resident White Woman, Lisa Bond, for her take:

"I've said before that white supremacy is the ultimate grift. It always has been—and it relies on constantly changing fads to feed its never-ending appetite.

"Take the current white wellness and self-help craze.

"Now, I'm not saying all life coaching is bad. I know some amazing life coaches that have antiracist and decolonized centers and do amazing work with their clients. I'm also not saying that wellness and self-help are not important—in fact, both of these things are incredibly important, ESPECIALLY as we work on unlearning and decolonizing.

"However, when you can get a 'life coach certificate' in three days and start profiting off white supremacy, well . . . I just tend to question it.

"So much of the white life-coaching, self-help, wellness industry requires that white women feel inadequate within the current systems. **It relies on our being oppressed but doesn't allow us to see the ways in which we oppress.** These programs, if not centered in abolition and decolonization, rely heavily on the trauma of white supremacy culture and reactivate it with . . . more white supremacy."

So what does Lisa mean by "trauma of white supremacy culture"? Recall your need to be perfect—an objectively impossible task, trying for something over and over that is unattainable. You feel like a perpetual failure. That is trauma. You are never thin enough, smart enough, successful enough, sexy enough, a good enough wife, mother, daughter, *person*. That is trauma. Your need to be nice, which leads to silence. You are silent when you are abused by men and each other. Trauma. You are silent when you abuse us. Trauma. You take abuse at work at the hands of each other and men. Trauma. You abuse us at work. Trauma. You were raised to be violent and you are raising racist kids to be every bit as violent as you. Generations of trauma—to us, yes . . . but also to you.

Most white life coaches capitalize on this trauma, knowing that you essentially feel like shit about yourselves. You have a bad body image, you feel disempowered, and you're lacking self-esteem. Your trauma, created by white supremacy culture, is their arbitrage opportunity.

And you fall for it, Like, subscribe, and link in bio.

So how do these white grifters replace your existing trauma borne of white supremacy culture with more white supremacy culture? The primary message of self-care and self-improvement gospel is that you alone are responsible for your own happiness. It's meant to be empowering, but it negates the huge impact that systems and structures—outside of our control—have on our personal fates. The toxic positivity of white wellness says that "success is 99 percent attitude and 1 percent aptitude," but this ignores the reality of systemic racism. A positive attitude cannot end the oppression Black, Indigenous, and brown women experience. So who are your white wellness heroines speaking to? YOU. JUST YOU. And if you are focused simply on making your white selves "braver" to stand up to your husband or male colleague, all you are doing is attempting to be more like that dude. Here's that gender lens again. This is white feminism at work. You will recall that white feminism supports white supremacy.

There is a place for personal accountability, certainly. But white wellness ideology does not heal the trauma of white supremacy culture ("I'm not good enough, I should be more successful, I need to have more . . . do more . . . be more"); instead, it replaces it with toxic individualism: "It's all up to me. I am responsible for everything that happens. Choose my happiness. Be my best. I *can* get more . . . I *can* do more . . . I *can* be more. Me. Me. ME."

White women who have embraced and internalized these ideals cannot help but then project them onto others. They project this mindset onto other white women. And, even more harmful, they project it onto Black, Indigenous, and other women of color. It places the onus for progress and improvement on an individual, and it erases the need for systemic change, obscuring the white supremacy that harms marginalized groups.

Here's the thing: white supremacy cannot thrive in community. White life-coaching and self-help work does not build community—it builds individualism. It's a grift packaged as a tool of success. White self-help doesn't really promote wellness. It promotes individualism within the confines of the system. It promotes elitist—entitled—wellness. How so? White wellness isn't concerned with systemic wellness—things like eradicating poverty or building adequate housing or establishing free health care or ending hunger or abolishing injustice. White wellness doesn't promote wellness beyond self. Communal wellness is not a thing in these circles because communal wellness requires us to *really* look within.

"And it works beautifully on us white women because we don't like ourselves," says Lisa Bond. "That's why white supremacy is such a grift. We pay others to help us like ourselves, and when it comes down to it—we just end up painting over shit because life coaching isn't about unlearning white supremacy. It's just about relearning the same thing in different ways."

Pay close attention to this: dismantling your racism isn't about learning something new. It is about unlearning that which you know deeply. No matter how many times you meditate or how many cleanses you do, you cannot escape the fact that you have been programmed to be racist.

The goal is to unlearn it and unknow it. And white influencers, healers, and coaches are not going to show you the path to unlearning white supremacy.

"Spiritual gangsters" are white wolves in culturally appropriated clothing.

It is easy to buy and consume—and the wellness and self-help industry is always selling you something. What's difficult is to interrupt your whiteness. It's hard to say no to perfection. It's hard to take a stand against racism in your home or your workplace. It's hard to tell your kids the truth about our history, our reality, your white privilege, their white privilege.

"We hate ourselves," Lisa Bond says. "We hate ourselves and we hate you. We hate you because we can see that you, Black, Indigenous, and other women of color, don't hate yourselves." White women have the luxury of self-hatred because of their white privilege. Black, Indigenous, and other women of color cannot afford self-hatred; it is too much, on top of the hatred the rest of the world has for us.

White supremacy keeps you in constant competition with yourself—and each other—and us. But your self-help idols and girl boss influencers profit off encouraging you to be even more self-destructive through this abject individualism and toxic positivity that is making you less healthy, less happy, and more dangerous to us—and to yourselves.

CHAPTER NINE

White Allies, White Saviors, White Violence.

"I am an ally" is something we hear from white women *all the time*. On social media. Over Zoom. In real life, at real dinners.

This comes as no surprise considering white women's quest to be perfect, to be nice, to be *good*. Next to the downward dog, white allyship is the white woman's favorite pose.

Of course, you can't just *be* an ally, you need to get credit for it. You need everyone to know, which is why you are all over social media talking about your allyship—and telling us about your allyship every chance you get.

So, what is a white ally?

Here's our definition: a white person who tries to stand side by side with BIPOC against white supremacy, racism, and xenophobia. A white person who thinks they are doing the right thing, on the right side of history. A well-intentioned white person.

Sounds good in theory. In practice, it often sucks.

The impact of your actions always outweighs your intentions. And yet you are so wedded to your good intentions that you are unable to see how your actions are harmful even when we tell you that they are. To your face. Repeatedly.

Not long ago, Lacy, a white woman who'd been following us on social media, commenting here, there, everywhere, hashtagging her #allyship, got triggered by one of our Facebook posts. We had asked folks to comment with an adjective that best described white women. The adjectives came in fast and furious from Black, Indigenous, brown, *and* white women. As you might imagine, some white women became enraged that negative adjectives were being used to describe "all white women."

Lacy was one of them. She wasn't just upset, she was *irate*. How was this useful? What were we trying to achieve? She used to be a supporter of ours, but now she understood why white women hated us. Despite myriad attempts by myriad people, including us, asking her to stop her violent responses, she kept going. And got worse.

It was as though she broke her allyship seal and all the racism, the xenophobia, the misogynoir came bursting out. The #whiteally hashtag was a flimsy dam holding back a sea of unmitigated hate.

She kept going and going and going.

Crazy part? We knew Lacy, in real life. We used to not only frequent her local business, but actively supported it by sending all kinds of folks her way. After all, her storefront was wallpapered in signs: BLACK LIVES MATTER, EVERYONE IS WELCOME HERE, HATE HAS NO HOME, and rainbows. So many rainbows, all of which led to a pot of hate.

We texted her to stop. Emailed her to stop. Other "white allies" did the same. She continued for days and days on Facebook, attacking other women of color.

It was wild.

And she still wouldn't stop. She started trashing us all over town, calling us "grifters," which is what several actual white supremacists and Nazis have called us on social media. She started engaging in digital conversations with these hatemongers, mostly white men with a smattering of white women.

Lacy, the great white ally, was openly in bed with white supremacists against us, Black and brown women, *all because we asked folks to list adjectives to describe white women.*

In response, she had basically fulfilled every negatively associated adjective that had been listed.

Eventually Lacy got bored, or more accurately, she felt relief and peace after unleashing her violence on a bunch of Black, Indigenous, and brown women. This is classic abuser behavior.

Her storefront, of course, is still painted with Black Lives Matter graphics and rainbows.

Her social media feed (we are told; we obviously had to block her) is still filled with hollow statements of white allyship, still boasting about her racial justice work in the community.

Lacy is a terrific example of how white allies can be the most dangerous kind of white person. Another dangerous example of a well-meaning white person is the white savior. To be clear, white allies and white saviors are not mutually exclusive. You can be, and often are, both.

A white savior is a white person who "comes to the aid" of a Black, Indigenous, or brown person. In the mind of a white savior, they are doing good, noble work, even God's work.

You are saving us.

Bear in mind:

White people have created the system of white supremacy. White people benefit from white supremacy. YOU have both created and benefit from the very thing you are purportedly saving us from.

Read that again.

You create the violence. You benefit from the violence. You then "save" us from the violence, and even when we tell you your purported "good deeds" are causing more harm, you continue.

Let's use an example that centers misogyny and sexism, something that might resonate more easily with you as a white woman.

Think of the "good guy" syndrome, the guy, we'll call him Drew, at your office who is always commiserating with you about what a sexist place it is, always the first to say, "We need more women in this office," who posts stories about sexism in the workplace on LinkedIn and Facebook, the one who wants you to see what a good and decent man he is, the one who will trash other "sexist men" behind their backs to gain points with you. He wants nothing more than for you to see what an ally he is to women. To you. To show you how he is saving you and the handful of other women from the toxic masculinity of your office.

What is Drew not doing? He is not working to actually dismantle toxic masculinity. He is not stepping aside and pulling you up into a position of power. Maybe even stepping aside to allow a woman to take his C-suite role. Screaming and yelling to flip the board to one that is majority woman. Speaking up publicly, in real time, in meetings as sexist things are said and done.

Drew is working to look like a prince within the system from which he benefits. Likely at the expense of other men: winking and nodding behind closed doors to you about what a douche John is, or how he totally heard that Paul is a sexual harasser. You see him as a friend, a safe harbor in an otherwise dangerous sea of misogyny.

Drew is doubly rewarded: once by the patriarchy, twice by the optics of being better than other men within the patriarchy.

Finally, what if you even asked Drew to stop? If you told him that his words and actions have had the adverse effect of making life worse for you and the other women at work. That the culture has become more oppressive, more sexist. And he still won't stop. Because stopping would require him to stop performing, he would lose his prime role, center stage—and that's all he wanted in the first place.

This same logic applies to you and white saviorism.

We use this example to ensure you white women understand that white saviors are not just Sally Struthers in Africa. White saviors are, in fact, performative, so there is little difference between white saviors and performative white allies.

White saviorism is so embedded in our cultural psyche that you might not even realize it. Remember that white cocoon?

Because it is so ubiquitous—like air—you likely don't see it. To be fair, you come by it honestly. Your entire childhood . . . your whole existence . . . you've been fed hundreds of feel-good flicks designed to get your white savior juices flowing.

Some of your favorite movies are white savior movies.

To Kill a Mockingbird—going back to 1962.

Atlantis: The Lost Empire—an animated savior movie for the kids!

The Help—for white women.

Green Book—for middle-aged white men.

City of Joy—for missionaries and international white folks.

Dances with Wolves—for colonizers who like the "Wild West."

The Blind Side—for white and especially white transracial adoption families.

Every genre, every age group, every decade, white people are fed the lies of white saviorism. Then you go out of your home and you relive these lies at the expense of Black, Indigenous, and brown people across the country and around the globe.

Here's a real-life example from the Race2Dinner event we described in the preface—the one with two white women who were volunteers at Love Colorado, a "social justice nonprofit." They said it would be *impossible* for them to be racist because they volunteer at this organization every week.

They talked over us. They rolled their eyes at us. They crossed their arms, pushed their chairs back. In every way possible, they made it known that they thought we were wrong.

They argued, repeatedly, for the entire two hours, that *because* they gave their time and money to organizations that fought for racial justice, it was impossible for them to be racist.

They went on to speak about how much time they spend with Love Colorado, working hands-on with Black and brown people.

Too many hours to count.

You both have no idea how many people we help.

We were even invited to Ronny's daughter's wedding. They love us. (Ronny is one of the many Black people they have "helped.")

This is what the white savior complex looks like in everyday life. This is the real-life version. They take their good deeds to social media as well. Photographs of soup kitchens, marches, protests, their kids' bake sales for Black Lives Matter, lemonade stands to Stop Asian Hate, and—for those white saviors with enough money to travel internationally—pictures of themselves building houses for poor Black, Indigenous, and brown people in Africa, Asia, and Central America.

Even when we pointed out that volunteering and donating to causes does not absolve you from being racist, they kept going.

They know. They know what's best for us. After all, they are white. And you know, white people know what's best for everyone, including us folks of color.

A few months later, Saira met a young Latino man who perked up when she told him she was one half of Race2Dinner. We will call him Alex. Alex is a staff member at Love Colorado who mentioned that these two white women volunteers were trashing Saira and Regina all over town, to anyone who'd listen, including him. He told them to stop, that it made him deeply uncomfortable to be asked to take the side of white women over Black and brown women when it came to the subjects of racism and xenophobia. He'd asked his boss to be removed from any scenario where he'd have to interact with them directly.

Let's recap.

1. White women deny their racism to Black and brown women.

2. The white women use their good deeds and dollars as evidence that they aren't racist.

3. When Black and brown women tell them this cannot be the case, the white women fight back. They belittle, talk down, deny, gaslight, tone police.

4. They leave and go into the world and trash the Black and brown women to others, including other BIPOC in an attempt to pit us against each other.

These women are classic white saviors. Rather than think to yourself how horrible they are and assure yourself you have nothing in common with them, take some time to really interrogate all the instances in which you may have acted as a white savior.

Trust us, they are legion.

It should be noted that white saviors who get called out for bad behavior almost always weaponize their dollars, making it known that their financial "help" and "support" is conditional on our unconditional adulation of them. This is why white philanthropy is, for the most part, a witches' brew of white women and white saviorism. You snatch those dollars back the minute you feel unappreciated or, God forbid, under attack for something you've said or done. In other words, you have us dancing for dollars. Something you are familiar with, considering you do the same at the feet of white men. Not calling out sexism for fear of losing your job or losing funding for your nonprofit. What white men do to you (and us), you do to us.

Here is what Lisa Bond has to say about white saviorism: "One of the things I have noticed about us white women—even when we engage in what we think is antiracism work, is how we frame it. For instance, the way we use the word 'help.' It has taken me what feels like ages to understand how and why we use this word. What is the message behind it? The reality is we believe the action we are taking is not for us. Which means we do this work outside of ourselves. Which means, honestly, that we have not learned (1) how we uphold white supremacy and (2) that we, too, are harmed by white supremacy. Help is a poor substitute for liberation."

Help is charity. If you don't feel tied to the fight, you will see your work as charity. If you don't feel tied to the fight, you will feel empowered to duck in and out of the work at your leisure. You will easily succumb to your feelings, your fatigue, your desire to "just enjoy the holidays." Until and unless you see your life in this fight, you will continue to see your work as help—you will continue to be a white savior. And white saviors are white supremacists in action.

White supremacy is a construct invented to allow for the oppression of others. White supremacy, as we have noted repeatedly, hurts not just us, but also you. White people.

You might be wondering how you can benefit from something that is harming you. The short answer: Your whiteness gives you privileges—advantages—that Black, Indigenous, and brown folks do not enjoy. Advantages in every possible way. From food to housing to education to health care to financial security to body autonomy and everything in between.

Yet your whiteness also harms you, something we've attempted to show you throughout this book. Your whiteness is preventing you from being in authentic community with other people. Your whiteness prevents the rest of us from living our fullest lives. Regina always says, "Imagine if the person who is going to cure cancer is sitting in a concentration camp at our border or in jail." Your whiteness denies our humanity and, in turn, prevents you from being fully human yourself.

Your whiteness is robbing ALL of us.

Therefore, in order for us to be free and live to our fullest potential, we must eradicate white supremacy.

Do you see now how your liberation is tied to our liberation? How your fight against white supremacy cannot be "help" or "support" or *allyship*? That fighting against white supremacy is fighting for YOU and YOUR KIDS, not just us and our kids?

You need to be *in* the fight, not helping. To help is to be ancillary, to be outside the problem. You are the center of the problem. Allies don't have any skin in the game; they are standing side by side in solidarity. But you *do* have skin in the game—your white skin. Stop aspiring to be an ally—and good Lord, stop calling yourself an ally. Rather, be an accomplice. A partner, a collaborator, a coconspirator. Anything but an ally.

The fight against white supremacy is not just a fight for Black, Indigenous, and brown people. This is a fight for your life, your children's lives, and for Mother Earth.

White supremacy is killing us all.

Now we're asking you to get up and fight because your lives—and ours—depend on it.

Epilogue

Nearly nine months go by and we meet again with Lauren, Lynn, and Elizabeth, the women who hosted the dinner described at the beginning of the book, in "The Rules" section. This time it's during a global pandemic, so we meet over Zoom, not dinner.

We've learned that the dinner came together like this: Elizabeth provided the guests—they were her friends and acquaintances. Lynn knew Elizabeth from previous racial justice work and offered up her house. As for Lauren, she'd caught wind of Race2Dinner on Facebook and contacted the white woman on our team, who paired her with Lynn and Elizabeth.

"I didn't really know anyone there and couldn't believe the rampant narcissism," Lauren tells us emphatically, the evening still jangling her nerves despite the passing of three seasons. "It ended up being all the worst-case scenarios. It was wild. When I stepped in, the other white women didn't talk over me and throw a bunch of white savior bullshit in my face the way they did the two of you. I was treated very differently when I spoke up."

Elizabeth agrees. "It was a disaster. I was embarrassed, confused, pissed, and surprised."

Lynn emphasized this. "Our guests did everything I told them not to do. I made a point to tell them not to give a civil rights introduction. We had told them to come prepared to explain why they were there. What they wanted to learn," she says, shaking her head. "I told them, 'We are not interested in your pedigree. I know it's not easy. You want to be accepted and to show you aren't like the others.' They didn't read *White Fragility*. They came in cold."

Lynn, Elizabeth, and Lauren are intensely critical of the other white women but save their harshest criticism for themselves. When asked what stood out as the biggest surprise, the most shocking thing of the night, they each tell us the same thing: "my silence," or what Elizabeth refers to as "white quiet."

Although time doesn't heal all wounds when it comes to racism (see America's *entire* history), time can provide the space necessary for change. It seems to have done so in the cases of Lynn, Elizabeth, and Lauren.

"I now speak up. I've learned to speak up," Lynn says. "It took Saira coming to get me out of the kitchen to see, in that one moment, all the damage that I've created in a lifetime. I now take risks and speak up."

"Yeah," Lauren adds, "I've become a better listener and have inherently shifted the way I communicate openly. I don't feel like I have to censor myself as I've become educated in the white privilege experience." She pauses before adding, "But I still float through my life with ease. It doesn't change the way the world perceives me. I'm still white."

For Elizabeth, her silence from that night has dogged her, a constant reminder to do better. "What happened at that dinner blew me away. I assumed I knew these women along these lines, being able to sit in a room like that with each other and you two. I am more self-aware about my whiteness, particularly around not speaking up. I know that my quiet is a promotion or agreement of whatever racist thing is said."

As to whether they'd call themselves racist now, for all three it is a resounding yes. Although Elizabeth reminds us that she'd raised her hand on that fateful night. She knew then. She's known for a long time.

The biggest shift seems to be an internalized understanding that being racist doesn't automatically mean you are "bad." It's the result of being a white American in this country. This is a critical step of the work. If you're stuck on feeling bad, you're stuck on centering your feelings.

Feeling bad snuffs any sparks of progress; feeling bad suggests impotence and enables you to uphold white supremacy. Back to an example many of you will understand more easily.

Let's say that you tell your father, your male partner, or even a male friend that they are behaving in sexist ways, but rather than get angry and defensive, they wallow in how bad they feel.

They feel *so* bad.

This, too, like anger and defensiveness, is a product of fragility. Male fragility.

Similarly, when white women get bogged down in guilt and shame, it derails the work. You are consumed by your own shame, rather than being consumed with the hard work of examining your racism—and thinking through how to be better. This is why white guilt is every bit as dangerous as white anger.

"I more thoroughly understand the systemic part. I've stopped taking it personally but take the responsibility of dismantling my own racism and holding up the mirror for others to do the same very seriously," Lauren explains evenly.

"So many of us live in a white bubble. It was designed that

way. It's diabolically ingenious," Lynn says, laughing a bit (you'll recall that white cocoon we discussed earlier). "There is a clarion call and we have to step out of our white bubble. It's destroying our country and the world. It's the source of global warming because of how we run industry. Even in our own homes, the things we choose to buy, the way we treat our neighborhoods, and the way we keep people out of our neighborhoods—how we sell our houses and who the buyers are going to be. Every one of our actions could be changed to support racial justice."

Elizabeth adds a crucial point about empathy: it is important, when embarking on antiracism work with other white women, to have empathy. "We can't approach this work with our typical white arrogance. The I-know-how-to-do-this-and-you-need-to-follow-along way. Instead, I'll share what's worked for me and you can share what's worked for you. Let's work together rather than [this attitude of] 'you really need to be a good student of mine.'"

During our chat with Lynn, Lauren, and Elizabeth, one thing becomes clear: a critical change has occurred.

That change is awareness. Awareness of their whiteness. Awareness of their silence, a chronic silence that's defined their lives. A chronic silence that's aided and abetted racism, letting it flourish at school, at work, at the dinner table, in Sunday school, while dating, while married, while divorced, while parenting.

While breathing.

And this awareness enables them to start being less afraid of confronting the truth about their complicity in white supremacy, racism, and xenophobia.

Now is a good time to talk about fear.

White supremacy culture cannot exist without white fear. Fear of being in the minority, losing power and privilege, being treated by BIPOC people the way you've treated us, being called racist, getting "canceled," saying or doing the wrong thing, and in the case of white women, fear of social, professional, or personal loss. We've heard stories of this happening.

"I publicly wrist slapped our neighbor for referring to something as 'ghetto' at a potluck once, and my kids were left out of Halloween in the neighborhood."

"My husband will literally leave me if I call out his racist parents at Thanksgiving."

"It took me a decade to climb the ranks at work. If I start barking about the coded racist things my colleagues say, that'll be it for me."

What we heard from Lynn, Elizabeth, and Lauren is that they felt less afraid to take this work on.

"You just have to open your eyes and see the wake you're creating behind your white bubble," says Lynn. "We create this wake of destruction behind us, and we don't look back."

At least these three women, *for now*, are looking forward, side to side, and back.

It's the beginning, not the end. The essential beginning to a lifelong journey to dismantle a racism so insidious it's baked into their DNA.

You have to start somewhere.

For this book, we reached out to Nicole to see how things have gone in the six months since our dinner in Chicago, the one where she acknowledged having been silent when her white male doctor boss made a comment about wanting to hire fewer "foreign doctors."

"I was doing rounds, talking to providers and nurses, and we just had a white guy who was COVID positive and had spent a lot of time at the hospital. The white nursing director, Beth, relays to me that this patient tells her he has concerns with people getting COVID, especially with the protests happening, and that rolled into him making a comment. 'When I lived through the sixties, I understood what they were fighting for, but now I don't know what they are fighting for.' Many of the conversations I've had at work have been related to the protests. Beth said to me, 'I have to say that I agree with him.'"

The protests of which she speaks are the ones that took place around the world after Derek Chauvin, a white police officer, murdered George Floyd on May 25, 2020.

Nicole speaks quickly and furiously. So much so that we have to ask her to slow down. She takes a deep breath and continues.

"In that moment, I said, 'Tell me more about that,' because I wanted to hear her thoughts. She really didn't understand. She thought racism was in the past. I said, 'Beth, I have to stop you there. Because there is serious systemic racism still at play in this country.' So I turned to COVID as an example. We have a pandemic, structural racism, and health disparities, and I led her through that. I said, 'Why has COVID affected more people of color than white people?' and I walked her through it."

Nicole tells us how the book *So You Want to Talk about Race* by Ijeoma Oluo has had a profound impact on her as well. Since having read it, she is laser-focused on her "intentions" when engaging fellow white people on racism. Namely, she enters these conversations knowing exactly what she wants to accomplish on the other end. In the case of the above conversation with Beth, Nicole's intention matched the outcome.

"By the end of the conversation, there was a little bit of a lightbulb moment for her. It has opened the door with Beth to have more discussions about the effects of structural racism against people of color."

We are delighted to hear that Nicole has stayed true to what she publicly stated at our dinner months earlier. That she has broken her silence.

Little by little. Step by step.

You have to start somewhere.

Glossary

1. **BIPOC:** Black, Indigenous, and people of color.

2. **people:** What white people say when they mean "white people," because white people think they are the default.

3. **white people:** White people.

4. **America:** A country founded on the genocide of Indigenous people, the enslavement and genocide of African people, and thereafter a spin cycle of racism and xenophobia, including but not limited to the Chinese Exclusion Act, Operation Wetback, Jim Crow, the Muslim ban, the Department of Homeland Security.

5. **critical race theory:** The truth about American systemic racism that is not taught in schools but that white people claim is taught in schools to terrify other white people that their white children will learn the truth about their complicity in racial violence past, present, and future.

6. **white supremacy:** The lie created by white people that white people are better and therefore the default. Common misconception:

white supremacists are just the Ku Klux Klan, Nazis, Republicans. Reality: all of our society is predicated on white supremacy, which is why you call yourselves "people" rather than "white people" and you refer to non-white folks as "diverse."

7. **whiteness:** Whiteness is the very construct that allows white supremacy to flourish. It is the lie that creates the norms. And like any good lie, it changes regularly to fit the wants, needs, and desires of white people. Example of whiteness: white people taking offense at the term "white people" because white people think they are simply "people," the default.

8. **white privilege:** The benefits of having white skin, which is, in short, white supremacy.

9. **white feminism:** Seeing everything through a gender lens, erasing other marginalized identities, including race. For example, you see your oppression as a woman, rather than your power as a WHITE woman. Famous white feminists: Susan B. Anthony, Nancy Pelosi, Sheryl Sandberg, *Sex and the City.*

10. **Karen:** All white women, especially white women who do not think they are Karens.

11. **"not all white women":** Your attempt to exempt yourselves from the toxic behavior of white people who openly do awful, racist things. Commonly stated by white women in real life and on social media every time a "Karen video" goes viral. "Oh my God, look at that Karen" rather than noticing all the ways you are very much like that Karen. *See also* Karen, white fragility, white nonsense.

12. **white fragility:** White people's hurt and angry feelings when racism and, more specifically, your racism are brought up. Your feelings trump the discussion, shutting down the discussion at best, and at

worst, punishing the person, usually a person of color, for bringing up the discussion. *See also* "not all white women," Karen, your feelings.

13. White Women Tears: Your proclivity to cry when faced with discussions on racism, particularly discussions on your racism. *See also* white fragility, white nonsense, your feelings.

14. your feelings: The elevation of your feelings over all else, including the reality of racism for BIPOC. This includes putting a stop to any conversations you deem to be "hard" and manipulating others into being responsible for your not doing the required inner work. Common usage: "You hurt my feelings." *See also* white fragility, "not all white women," Karen, gaslighting.

15. diverse people, diverse candidates, diverse books: What white people mean when they are referring to people, candidates, and books that are not white. It assumes default people, candidates, and books are white or white-centered.

16. diversity, equity, and inclusion (DEI): What companies, institutions, and organizations call their efforts to do nothing about racism, while checking boxes. Often led by a white woman.

17. colorblind: Something white people call themselves to indicate how not racist they are while actually exposing themselves as the real racists. *See also* "I am not racist."

18. ally: Something white women often call themselves, which usually indicates they are anything but an ally. *See also* white savior.

19. accomplice: Something to which white women should aspire. Never a moniker to bestow upon oneself, but a practice indicating that you see your liberation and your life as tied to the liberation and lives of Black, Indigenous, and brown folks. We are fighters in the same war against white supremacy, a war that you must win for your own sake and not a pet project that you support and help during your downtime.

20. **"crazy busy":** Something white women often call themselves to indicate just how busy they are with life, work, kids, family. Translation: "I am busier than you." Reality: It is an excuse not to fight against injustice, because you simply do not have the time. It centers you and your lives over everyone else's, assuming we are not humans who also have life, work, kids, bills to pay, sick elderly parents to care for.

21. **gaslighting:** White people's foolish—and evil—mental trick to make BIPOC think we are imagining racism, making up racism, over-reacting to racism. A way to erase our experience while making us feel "crazy." *See also* white people.

22. **"I am married to a Black/Asian/Indigenous/Latino person":** You use this as dispositive proof that you cannot be racist. Reality: you cannot fuck your way out of racism. *See also* White Woman Bingo.

23. **"I am not racist":** A statement made by white people that we hear as "I am very racist." *See also* colorblind.

24. **"listening and learning":** A white euphemism for "I already know and don't care."

25. **microaggression:** White acceptable term for the bullshit racist words and behaviors you use to demean BIPOC in your effort to subtly maintain your superiority. There is nothing "micro" about the hate you give.

26. **nice:** Something white women aspire to, which means smiling to your face and stabbing you in the back.

27. **perfection:** A white woman's goal in life. As an objectively unattainable goal (perfection is impossible), what it means in reality is

feeling like shit your whole life for not being pretty, smart, thin, success-ful, or wealthy enough and competing with all other women to get as close to your vision of perfect as possible. Whiteness is a foundational principle of perfection, so Black, Indigenous, and brown women are ren-dered imperfect from birth. Perfection keeps you in competition with yourselves—and each other—to all of our detriment.

28. Performative Activism or Performative Allyship: When your antiracism work is geared towards looking nice, getting a hug or a pat on the back, and being perfect rather than actually wanting to dismantle white supremacy. Common Performative Activists: White women on Facebook and Instagram compulsively sharing antiracism memes, Liking and sharing posts while doing nothing in their real lives. White women who head up DEI departments.

29. spiritual bypassing: The toxic and emotionally stunted process of avoiding discussions about racism and feelings of anger, resentment, embarrassment, and jealousy by entering the spiritual realm of Distance and Avoidance. For example, see toxic positivity.

30. tone policing: When you focus on the tone of what we are saying, rather than the substance of what we are saying, typically when we are talking about your racism. It is a tactic to deflect from the conversation you do not want to have. A tactic to evade accountability. White women are the classic tone police, first responders on the scene when BIPOC call out your bad behavior.

31. toxic positivity: A white woman's need to brightside everything, which requires sidelining and erasing talk of oppression. For example: "Love trumps hate" and "I choose to see the good rather than focus on the bad." *See also* spiritual bypassing, white nonsense, white woman wellness.

32. white nonsense: All levels of ridiculous explanations and de-fenses you have for validating unacceptable white racist behaviors. Common example: you.

33. white savior: White people who revel in "rescuing" BIPOC. You want to be seen as heroes, "helping" those beneath you rather than fighting for racial justice because (a) it is the right thing to do and (b) your white lives depend on dismantling white supremacy too. Famous white saviors: Sally Struthers, the song "Do They Know It's Christmas?," Mother Teresa, white women on Instagram and Facebook.

34. White Urgency: Your need to be involved *immediately* when racial violence is exposed. You were the first to demand answers about racism and antiracism in the aftermath of George Floyd's murder. You were also the first to lose interest once it became clear that antiracism is a lifelong practice and journey and not a one-day sample sale.

35. white woman wellness: Entitled practices of self-care where white women ignore reality, become the most oppressed people on the planet, and learn to dial into their "inner white man." Famous examples: Glennon Doyle, Gwyneth Paltrow, Rachel Hollis.

36. White Woman Bingo: When you hit multiple toxic white woman behaviors in one sitting. For example: Not All White Women, Your Tone Is a Turnoff, That Hurts My Feelings, White Women Tears, I'm Listening and Learning, I Am Married to a Black Man.

37. white woman proverbs: You Hurt My Feelings, Be Nice, I'm Listening and Learning, I Don't Like Your Tone, My Best Friend Is Black.

38. White Woman Woke Wars: Your need to be perfect means you have to be the best at everything, including antiracism work. You will claw each other's eyes out to appear to be THE most antiracist. You try to one-up other white women with Facebook and Instagram photos of you holding signs and marching, your kids selling cookies for Black Lives Matter and Stop Asian Hate, you with your token Black, Indigenous, or brown friend here, there, everywhere. *See also* Performative Activism, perfection, white nonsense.

39. cultural appropriation: White people wearing our cultures and ethnicities like a costume. White people using our cultures and ethnicities for profit. Common examples: white people on Halloween, white yoga instructors, Ariana Grande.

40. token Black, Indigenous, or brown friend: The one Black, Indigenous, or brown "friend" to whom you refer when your racism is called out. Common usage: "My friend Zoe is Black and she doesn't think I'm racist!" We implore you to resist your white urge to call, text, or email Zoe or any of your other BIPOC friends when reading this book to get their approval that you are not like the white women described in the preceding pages. You are. And Zoe is tired.

Acknowledgments

First and foremost, immeasurable gratitude to all the Black, Indigenous, and brown women who shared their pain with us for this book: Shana V. White, Kristin Mink, Myriam, Rhea Rowan, Carmella Boykin, Marisol Solarte-Erlacher, Mariana del Hierro, Shireen Mitchell, Candi CdeBaca, Shay Stewart-Bouley, Nina Baliga, Dr. Tamara Lee, Xóchitl Gaytán, LadySpeech Sankofa, Cynthia P., and Preeti Mistry.

Thanks to the white women who were able to put aside their white nonsense to help make this book happen: Jess Regel, who sold it, Margaux Weisman, who bought it, and Ruth Ann Harnisch, who has committed to getting it into the hands of thousands of white educators. Thanks to another white woman, Patty Ivins Specht, who made Deconstructing Karen, a film about our work.

Thanks to everyone at Penguin Books who helped with this book, especially Annika Karody. Like every white institution in America, white supremacy lives in every nook and cranny of the publishing industry. Nobody is more surprised than us that Penguin actually published these pages.

Thanks to Lisa Bond, the white woman who is forever by our

side, dismantling her own bullshit while lighting the way for other white women.

Thanks to the Race2Dinner community. Many of you get knocked. Some of you get up again. Kudos.

Thanks to our family members and friends who aren't sick of us yet. There aren't many of you. You know who you are.

Love, respect, reverence, and gratitude to our ancestors. Without you, we wouldn't be here today.

Thanks to all the Black, Indigenous, and brown girls, women, and non-binary identify folks all over the world. We see you. We believe you. We are you.

Finally, these words at the end of every book are called "acknowledgments." Regina always says, "You can't change what you don't acknowledge." Asking all of you white women who made it this far: Can you acknowledge your white supremacy? Can you acknowledge how and when your racism shows up?

THOSE are the acknowledgments we'd like to see.

A Guide to Unlearning

A Conversation with Saira Rao and Regina Jackson

The book is centered on the Race 2 Dinner model, which has both of you moderating conversations between white women about racism and white supremacy. How is the book a tool for white women to confront their own racism, without you or other people of color holding them to account?

Saira: You can take a white woman to the water but you cannot force her to drink. Part of white supremacy culture is wanting everything handed to you on a silver platter—or in the case of antiracism work, wanting us to hold your hand, tell you what to do, and hand out cookies for a job well done. It just doesn't work that way. The work is messy. It is not linear. It requires you to dig deep and take your own personal journey. In other words, there are none of those boxes you adore checking.

Our job isn't to hold white women accountable. White women are grown-ass adults who need to hold themselves accountable, be in community with other white women who are deeply committed to antiracism work, and will hold each other accountable with love and kindness, rather than with the judgment, competition, and fake niceness that define white women's relationships with themselves and each other. We say at every dinner: start loving yourselves, start loving each other, start being in sisterhood with each other. Personal and community accountability—that's what white women need, not us Black, Indigenous, and brown women babysitting their antiracism work.

Regina: Part of R2D's work is creating coursework for white women to: 1. Understand white supremacy, what it is, how it functions, and how they uphold and benefit from it, and 2. Work in community with other white women and Black Indigenous Women of Color (BIWOC) to be accountable for doing the work. Third, we have also created coursework for BIWOC to live their best lives by creating a life map for taking control of their own lives and living without fear.

When did you realize that your silence would not protect you? How did it change your priorities?

Saira: I think I have always known that my silence would not protect me, but for most of my life, I leaned into my non-Black privilege and adjacency to whiteness as an Asian American. I would say it became glaringly obvious right after September 11. I was coming up the subway stairs into the World Trade Center that sunny Tuesday morning in 2001 and was one of the many people sprinting up Church Street when the towers fell. I left my apartment that day as a model minority and returned home as a would-be terrorist in the eyes of white America. I knew that day, with certainty, that my silence would not save me. It nevertheless took me years to find my voice.

Regina: It was not until I started my own business that I understood I did not have to tiptoe around white people's feelings. Many times, the truth is not pretty, but I am committed to being true to myself.

As you mention in the book, perfectionism and the lack of action and confrontation that result from it are a salient and oppressive feature of white supremacy. How have you maintained the energy and the motivation to continually confront instances of racism, both overt and subtle, in the face of a culture that would rather ignore it?

Saira: We are asked this question a lot: What keeps you going, how do you keep up the stamina? My answer is always the same: What choice do we have? White supremacy is killing us. All of us. When you see this clearly, and truly internalize what that means, you cannot not fight. My life, my children's lives, your life, and your children's lives all depend on each and every one of us interrogating white supremacy at every turn. The better question, I think, is what's keeping *you* from fighting tooth and nail for the only thing that matters in this world: our humanity.

Why aren't you mad as hell that police are murdering Black people and little kids are getting massacred at school and our tax dollars are going to fund white terrorists whipping Haitian people and destroying Afghanistan and THE EARTH? How are you able to sleep at night? Why do you have more energy and motivation to confront your Black coworker or Latino gardener or Asian manicurist for being late than you do to confront your own racist bullshit? WHY AREN'T YOU FIGHTING FOR YOUR LIFE AND YOUR CHILDREN'S LIVES?

Regina: I think what white people don't understand is that doing the work is not optional for us. You either do the work or you end up as someone's whipping boy. I have no interest in that position.

This book really is a "pulls no punches" kind of book. You even mentioned in your opening that some would put it down immediately. Why was it important for you to write this book in the most honest and direct way?

Saira: Even though white women try to tone police and gaslight us at every turn—*if you said it nicer; honey attracts more flies than vinegar*—we know it's not the way we are saying it, it is WHAT we are saying. Namely, that you all are racist. All white people are racist, just like all Asian Americans are anti-Black. We have all been put into the sausage factory, and when you go through the sausage factory you do, in fact, become a sausage. In America, the kind of sausage is based on your skin color. So white people, who are at the top of the food chain, are racist. Period. We can say it with a smile. We can say it while delivering them a pretty cake. We can say it while massaging their feet. And they would STILL hate it. So we might as well say it as clearly and simply and forcefully as we can, because they'll hate it regardless of how we say it.

As for the honesty part, white people's feigned ignorance of their racism is what keeps all this violence afloat. If you don't acknowledge the truth, you can continue to cause your racist harm with a clear conscience. By telling the truth—and beckoning white people to tell their own truth—this foundational feigned ignorance goes poof, and we can attempt to get somewhere.

Regina: For more than four hundred years Black people have been the recipients of violence, hate, rage, jealousy, and denial of our humanity under the legacy of white supremacy.

White people are the perpetrators of all of the above. I am tired of trying to convince them with morality, marches, demonstrations, and legislation, which frankly doesn't work unless we as a nation uphold our laws. It's time for every white person to look into the mirror, recognize the ways that they uphold centuries of hate, and make a commitment to themselves to just STOP causing other people pain and suffering because of the color of their skin.

Your work at Race2Dinner is centered on eight to ten white women at a time, yet the audience for this book is every white woman. Aside from the obvious "dinner party discussion," how does this book differ from the everyday work you do? How is it the same?

Saira: This book is very much an extension of our work. The obvious difference is that white women can (and will) easily walk away from the book. But aside from that, all of the feelings white women have while reading it—all of that internal dialogue— THAT is the stuff that comes out at our dinners: The deflection, the gaslighting, the exceptionalizing, and the virtue signaling that happens in EACH AND EVERY white woman's head? Every dinner. Every. Single. Dinner. White women are nothing if not consistent.

Regina: It differs in that a dinner can only impact a small number of people at a time, while this book can impact many thousands of people. The experiences will be the same: take no prisoners, look inside, tell the truth, and commit to change. Change only happens when staying the same is too uncomfortable to bear and is, therefore, no longer an option.

What is your favorite chapter or part of this book and why?

Saira: My favorite is Chapter 7: "Microaggressions" and How You Kill Us At Work. Your violence depends on gaslighting us, making us feel like it is us, as individuals, who are the problem: angry, divisive, not team players. By singling us out as the individual problems, you are able to deny the one gigantic systemic problem, namely WHITENESS and ALL WHITE INSTITUTIONS. In Chapter 7, we interview Black women, Indigenous women, Asian women, Latina women. They are in different parts of the country, in different professions, and the story is always the same: White women are horrible to work with. It turns your narrative on its head. We as individuals are not the problem—your whiteness is.

Regina: The chapter on white women and work. Because I can guarantee you that every woman of color has had to suffer through these unacceptable behaviors just to do the jobs that they were hired to do. It ranges from something as simple as someone thinking that you are too animated, to something as painful as someone else thinking that you dress too well for work. It's all nonsense and it is debilitating. Just STOP!

Throughout this book, you refer white women back to their own experiences with misogyny and sexism. Why?

Saira: By bringing it back to sexism, an oppression that white women experience, we clarify how their unwillingness to see their own racism is analogous to men's unwillingness to see their own sexism.

This unwillingness is caused by white feminism, which is the tendency of mainstream feminist theory, discourse, and practice to center gender oppression to the exclusion of racial oppression. You'll recall us talking about how white women will often say things like, "Well you don't get how it is to be a woman on the receiving end of sexism," as if we are not women too. We deal with sexism from white men and the men in our own communities, PLUS their white woman bullshit.

Let's be clear, white feminism is deadly. And it is pretty sad that we have to resort to making these constant comparisons to sexism for white women to see their violent ways. But we do. And it works.

Regina: White womens' experiences with misogyny and sexism give them a lens through which they can understand their own racist behavior. Their racism takes a similar form to the sexism leveled at them: put-downs, aggression, hostility, and righteousness. The only difference is that they are emboldened to act in these ways because of their race, as opposed to the element of gender that emboldens men to act the same way towards them.

In the preface you state: "We decided to write this book after more than a dozen dinners. Different white women, different dining rooms, different neighborhoods, different cities. SAME CONVERSATION. You are nothing if not consistently WHITE." What ways are white women NOT consistently white? Is that even possible?

Saira: Whiteness is whiteness. White womanhood is white womanhood. If the question is: Are there exceptional white women? I'd ask back: Why do we always have to exceptionalize white people? If the question is: Are there white women who are really and truly doing the work? The answer to that is: Yes. And it is white women who have no interest in being exceptionalized, praised, recognized as "not being consistently white," who are the ones doing the actual work. The ones who aren't asking us to teach them. They are seeking out resources on their own, they are finding community with each other, they are holding themselves and each other accountable, they are following many Black, Indigenous, and other women of color to get lots of perspectives. They are supporting radical, progressive candidates of color at every level. They are supporting Black-, Indigenous-, and brown-led businesses and nonprofits. And they are doing it without wanting us to throw them a parade.

They are doing it because they truly and deeply know that white supremacy is killing them too. And the only way to stop this violent death is through their personal daily actions.

So yes, plenty of white women are doing the work. They just aren't your favorite white woman Instagram influencer or white woman celebrity or white woman Silicon Valley girl boss.

Regina: It is possible, but it's only manifested by those who are committed to doing the inner work. This is not work where you attend a company-sponsored DEI session and you are good to go. This is work that requires you to be intentional about what you value in your life, to look in the mirror every day and decide to be an accomplice to antiracism, to listen to and accept guidance from Black and brown women, and to stop focusing on your feelings and centering yourself.

Questions for Discussion and Self-Accountability

PREFACE

What is the last thing you did or thought that was racist, that upheld systems and structures of white supremacy?

When you think about your life—from home, to work, to social—how do you see systems of white supremacy showing up?

CHAPTER ONE

Saira shared her story of white womanhood in this chapter. Knowing that you are not Saira, who are you in this story?

Perfectionism is a mirage. As you read this chapter, what were the ways that your own perfectionism arose in your innermost thoughts?

CHAPTER TWO

Regina shared her story about how she had to "be mean" to be kind. In what ways did that story make you uncomfortable? Recognizing that you are not Regina, who are you in this story?

White women are socialized to be the peacekeepers and to diffuse tension. When you think about your role at home, at work, and with your friends, how do you see this show up? What do you recognize 'behind the scenes'?

CHAPTER THREE

White silence is violence. This statement has been repeated often—on march signs and T-shirts—but has rarely been personally digested. Identify a time when you were silent that you now regret. What is preventing you from speaking to it now?

White supremacy and patriarchy are two sides of the same coin. How has your silence been carefully crafted in service to both?

CHAPTER FOUR

As white women, your lived experience cannot include a racially intersectional lens. As you think about the ways you have shown up in the fight for women's rights, what are the ways in which you have refused to consider how your own whiteness and racial privilege have impacted the civil rights and other movements by marginalized people?

As you read Saira's story about a white feminist political action committee, what did you feel? Who were you in this story? What are some ways that you think it could have evolved in a more inclusive fashion?

CHAPTER FIVE

Saira and Regina both shared personal stories in this chapter. As a refresher, Saira's story involved the white mother of one of her children's friends and Regina's involved a white woman policing yard signs. Name the reason it is easier for you to see yourself as the protagonist and then correctly identify why you would actually be the antagonist.

Your white entitlement is so normalized, it is often difficult to recognize the white supremacy within your everyday actions. In fact, most white women would deny that they ever engage in this behavior. Make a list of five entitled actions you recognize within yourself on a daily or semi-daily basis.

CHAPTER SIX

Think back to your education: elementary, secondary, postsecondary. How many Black, Indigenous, and non-Black teachers of color did you have? How do you think this impacted both the style and content of your education, and the way you live in the world today?

We know that there are entire industries built around the failure of Black, Indigenous, and non-Black students of color. How have you been complicit with this?

How have you shown up to ensure that schools in your area are engaging in the heavy work of decolonizing and antiracist education? What questions have you asked about the curriculum being accurate with respect to our history: regional, US, and global? What questions have you asked about the library resources? What questions have you asked of school leadership about the hiring of Black, Indigenous, and non-Black people of color?

CHAPTER SEVEN

This chapter shared multiple stories of Black, Indigenous, and non-Black women of color in the workplace. Which story's white woman antagonist is most like you? How? What are three ways that you can change that immediately?

We know that white women will statistically choose themselves and their advancement at work over their sisterhood with others, most especially Black, Indigenous, and non-Black women of color. Name at least one way you have stepped on another woman (and more specifically, a Black, Indigenous, and non-Black women of color) to advance or receive accolades. Within your own work context, name how you will prevent doing so in the future.

CHAPTER EIGHT

This chapter includes five definitions, with examples, of deflection techniques employed regularly by white women. Name at least one way you have engaged in each of these techniques to deflect from your own racism and complicity with white supremacy.

The grift of white supremacy goes hand in hand with the grift of white wellness. Take an inventory of the way you engage in platitudes, toxic positivity, and wellness culture. Name the ways in which your quest for enlightenment has actually been a study in white supremacy culture.

CHAPTER NINE

Name the ways in which you have made yourself the exception— giving yourself the title of ally or accomplice, when in reality you have acted in the capacity of a white savior. What do you see as the difference? How will this realization change you in the future?

How can you be an ally or a savior in the fight against something that also kills you? What are the ways in which white supremacy is hurting and killing us all? Going forward, what are the practical ways you will address white supremacy as a person who is both helped by and harmed by these systems?